UNIVERSITY OF MICHIGAN
MICHIGAN GOVERNMENTAL STUDIES
NO. 36

PUBLIC ADMINISTRATION AND THE PUBLIC— PERSPECTIVES TOWARD GOVERNMENT IN A METROPOLITAN COMMUNITY

BY

MORRIS JANOWITZ
Professor of Sociology
University of Michigan

DEIL WRIGHT
Assistant Professor of Political Science
Wayne State University

WILLIAM DELANY
Assistant Professor of Sociology
Cornell University

GREENWOOD PRESS, PUBLISHERS
WESTPORT, CONNECTICUT

Library of Congress Cataloging in Publication Data

Janowitz, Morris.
    Public administration and the public.

    Reprint of the 1958 ed. published by Bureau of
Government, Institute of Public Administration,
University of Michigan, Ann Arbor, which was issued as
no. 36 of University of Michigan, Michigan governmental
studies.
    Includes bibliographical references.
    1. Municipal government. 2. Public relations--
Municipal government. 3. Detroit--Politics and govern-
ment. I. Wright, Deil Spencer, 1930-   joint author.
II. Delany, William Thomas, 1923-   joint author.
III. Title. IV. Series: Michigan. University.
Bureau of Government. Michigan governmental studies ;
no. 36.
[JS89.J36 1977]   352'.008'0723   76-49866
ISBN 0-8371-9396-6

PREFACE

To REFER to a research report as exploratory has come to be a device for absolving the investigator from the responsibility of defending his findings. *Public Administration and the Public* is not, I trust, exploratory in this sense. The use of empirical techniques, however, to investigate the contacts, knowledge, and perspectives that the public has concerning administrative agencies has been an undeveloped research topic. This monograph is exploratory in that it seeks to deal with these problems from the point of view of public administration and social research.

I have sought, in addition, to analyze these empirical findings in the context of the American political process. The question can be raised whether these data help clarify the essential factors underlying the political democracy. Empirical research into the processes of political democracy has focused on the election system. Of course, what we have learned about evaluating elections is of relevance to public administration research. Thus, this monograph is an outgrowth of an earlier analysis[1] undertaken with my colleague Dwaine Marvick.

There we sought to develop and apply a series of criteria for judging whether the outcome of an election reflected a process of consent or the end product of mass manipulation. In this monograph, a series of criteria are developed and applied for judging whether the perspectives which the public holds toward administration are appropriate for a system of administration based on consent. Since there has been little formal thought in political science about this problem, these efforts must also be considered exploratory.

In preparing this research report, I have had the active collaboration of Deil S. Wright, Department of Political Science, Wayne State University, and William Delany, Department of Sociology, Cornell University, while they were in residence at the University of Michigan. Starting with differing

[1]Morris Janowitz and Dwaine Marvick, *Competitive Pressure and Democratic Consent* (Ann Arbor: Bur. of Government, Inst. of Public Administration, 1956).

political assumptions and theoretical disciplines, we worked to develop a common framework for analyzing public perspectives toward the administrative process. The body of data collected and analyzed deals with the impact of administration in a metropolitan community setting. As such, our findings may be of relevance to the growing reconsideration of metropolitan government in the life of American society.

Since our empirical efforts were based on the sample survey methodology, we are greatly indebted to a number of groups and individuals. The study was made possible because of the special facilities of the Detroit Area Study. The Detroit Area Study is a graduate training and research group of the University of Michigan which is associated with the Department of Sociology and the Survey Research Center. Special acknowledgement is due to Professor Ronald Freedman of the Department of Sociology for his leadership'in the development of this enterprise. During the academic year of 1953-54, when these data were collected, Dr. Morris Axelrod was the technical director of the Detroit Area Study. Both he and Dr. Harry Sharp, the current technical director, have been of continuous assistance. In fashioning the interview schedule, in interviewing the sample of 764 adults in the Detroit metropolitan community, and in coding the contents of the interviews the research assistants and the graduate students of the Detroit Area Study did their methodological apprenticeship. Because the Detroit Area Study is a unique approach to graduate training involving field participation, we worked with a research team of high esprit de corps and outstanding technical competence. The members of the group to whom grateful acknowledgements are due include:

Alden Anderson   Herbert M. Jackson
Lois Cartenson   Peter Kalinke
Richard Curtis   Marilyn Karlin
Basil Georgopoulos   Paul E. Kraemer
Oscar Grusky   Ilse Lubkes
Anne Hubbell   James Lynch
Charles H. Hubbell   Patricia Murphy Marion

Albert Meister	Ruth Searles
James Pifer	Joachim Seckel
Malcolm Roemer	Allan Silver
Michael Reuter	Sheila Gordon Zipf

In the analysis of empirical data, Deil S. Wright focused especially on the problem of the prestige of public employment. These findings are presented in Chapter V, The New Prestige of Public Employment. The full details of this aspect of the undertaking are presented in "The Prestige of the Public Service in a Metropolitan Community."[2] He was also closely connected with the analysis aspects of the entire effort. William Delany collected and analyzed the findings from the special sample of public servants in the Detroit metropolitan community designed to complement the representative sample. One aspect of these data supplies the basis of Chapter VII, Communicating to the Public: Barriers and Channels. The full research is reported in "Bureaucrat and Citizen: A Study of Government Bureaucracies in a Metropolitan Setting."[3]

Finally, I wish to acknowledge the sponsorship and support of this study by the Institute of Public Administration, University of Michigan, under its director, Professor John W. Lederle, and its associate director, Professor Ferrel Heady.

MORRIS JANOWITZ

[2]Unpublished Ph.D. dissertation, Univ. of Michigan, 1956.
[3]Unpublished Ph.D. dissertation, Univ. of Michigan, 1957.

CONTENTS

68179

I
PUBLIC PERSPECTIVES AND THE ADMINISTRATIVE PROCESS

THE IMMEDIATE problems of public administration require that social science research collect data which will complement the practical knowledge of the public administrator and his staff. For example, each administrator is concerned with what his clients, actual and potential, know and think about his agency since this information is important for internal administration. Without adequate public knowledge about the objectives of administrative progams, agency objectives are frustrated and the daily tasks of the administrator become immensely complicated. The administrator, of course, assumes that his day-to-day experiences give him a sensitive understanding of the awareness and demands of his clients and the public at large. But many administrators are continually seeking for additional sources of knowledge about their clients and it is the task of the social scientist to demonstrate to him that his knowledge can be increased by the use of systematic research.

Beyond these operational requirements, social science research ought to contribute to understanding the strategic consequences of administrative processes on contemporary society and democratic consensus. Public administrators, and students of government, whether they employ a pragmatic or a formal theory of administration, tend to view government organization in terms of its ability to resolve social and economic conflict. Again, social science research on public perspectives toward the organs of government is of relevance in helping to understand trends in social change.

This report presents an analysis of an empirical investigation of public perspectives toward specific administrative agencies as well as toward the administrative aspects of government in general. We assume that the task of supplying relevant data for the ongoing operations of public administrators and the task of understanding the consequences of public administration on our society are indeed compatible. The starting point of the investigation is a well-known observation. *The decisive transformation of modern government has been the growth in scope and power of government bureaucracy and the consequent problems which have been posed for the viability of democratic party politics.* In the language of Herman Finer, "This is the problem of the twentieth century: the relationship of officials and the public."[1]

Modern political theory continues, nevertheless, to emphasize elections as the crucial device for the democratic control of political power.[2] The election process has come to be seen as a device of popular sovereignty in that organized factions engage in competition. The public derives its power from the ability to choose periodically between political opponents who are claiming the right of temporary monopoly of political power. By contrast, a system of political theory which would outline the desired relations between government bureaucracy and the public in a democratic political system is relatively undeveloped.

Similarly, it is striking to note the extent to which contemporary political behavior research focuses on the election process to the exclusion of the administrative arena of power. The focus of the political behaviorist, however, does not seem to be a result of the state of political theory. Elections have been intensively studied because they lend themselves to the methodology of empirical research into politics. The election is a process of power politics which is characterized by finality of outcome, high popular involvement, and relative clarity of the essential procedures. It is a political event that is both discrete and periodic whereas many other aspects of the political process are amorphous and continous. These characteristics give the researcher the confidence that his mass-oriented research procedures, especially the sample survey, will produce significant results.

---

[1]Herman Finer, "Officials and the Public," *Public Administration*, IX (January 1931), p. 23.

[2]Joseph A. Schumpeter, *Capitalism, Socialism, and Democracy* (New York: Harpers, 1943); Pendleton Herring, *The Politics of Democracy* (New York: Rinehart, 1940); Robert A. Dahl, *A Preface to Democratic Theory* (Chicago: Univ. of Chicago Press, 1956); and Bernard Berelson, Paul Lazarsfeld, and William McPhee, *Voting* (Chicago: Univ. of Chicago Press, 1954).

Thus, the election process has served as a research site for analysis of the links between public perspectives and the political party system. Analysis of these perspectives and public involvement with administrative organization, however, remains at best an area investigated on a case study basis. This is due, in part, to the fact that research concerning the administrative process, like theory, has focused mainly on internal organization of individual agencies or on problems of interagency management. The efforts to professionalize public administration as a career have led to the development of a theory of public administration which is more a theory of management and less a theory of political power. The failure of the social scientist to investigate public perspectives toward the web of administration in broad fundamental terms is due, in part, to the fact that the administrative process is highly diffuse, highly segmental, and often indirect and has an essentially low visibility. The dramatic and periodic character which concretizes the election process is relatively absent as a basic focus for describing citizen attitudes and expectations about the public bureaucracy.

As a result of the imbalance in research interest between elections and the web of administration, the current trends in political behavior analysis present an incomplete picture of political attitudes and political values. Indeed, the imbalance may well have led to a distorted view of political consensus in American politics. The election is a process that emphasizes political cleavages, even though a wide range of political compromises becomes the basis for the final decision that each voter must make. The data collected during an election campaign, therefore, serve to highlight disagreements and dissensus. These data tend to emphasize feelings of protest and to chart the incompleteness and irrationality of political ideology. By analyzing public perspectives toward administration the extent and nature of underlying political consensus may emerge as quite different and more extensive than that observed in an election campaign.

To a degree which we never anticipated, the public's perspectives of the administrative process differed more within each political party than between the two parties. We developed our research scheme in the tradition of elections studies which seek to highlight the ideological differences between party adherents. Democratic identification and Republican identification, however, were insufficient as criteria for developing an effective understanding of the character and extent of consensus that exists toward the symbols of administrative authority.

A democratic society could not tolerate continuous election campaigning. Yet a democratic society must tolerate continuous administrative processes. There is no reason to suppose that the structure of sentiments mobilized and manifested during the heat of the campaign gives us a full picture of the public support on which administrative institutions must rest. Administrative behavior in a democratic society should tend to resolve social conflicts. Therefore, analysis of public perspectives toward the administrative process is essential to the formulation of a theory of public administration in a political democracy. This necessitates detailed empirical research into the public's contacts, attitudes, and evaluations of the agents and agencies of government. It also involves the development of a series of criteria for judging whether appropriate relations exist between the public bureaucracy and the citizenry.

THE CRITERIA: KNOWLEDGE, SELF-INTEREST, PRINCIPLE MINDEDNESS, AND PRESTIGE

From what standpoint can criteria be derived for judging whether the links between the web of administration and the citizenry are appropriate for a democratic political system? Either one of two standpoints can be taken. On the one hand there is the *internal* standpoint. The internal standpoint—the traditional public administration point of view—focuses attention on the internal organization of the public bureaucracy. Given this standpoint, a series of central questions emerge: what formal modes of organization, what rules of administration, what kinds of administrative personnel, what types of relationships with legislators and special interest groups are

most likely to facilitate the effective operations of the bureaucracy and ultimately render it responsible to its various publics
and to the electorate at large? Here the essential variables in administrative behavior are those relating to organization, management procedures, personnel, and immediate legislative relations.

On the other hand, the *external* standpoint seeks to analyze
links between the web of administration and the public by starting from the viewpoint of the public. The "public" is defined
as "all the clients of government subjected to various obligations
which they owe...to officials and entitled to the receipt of various services...from them."[3] Thus, the external standpoint, on
which this research is based, emphasizes the public and political
context in which public administration operates. It assumes
that the solution of internal administrative problems is dependent on an appropriate political climate in which administrative organization must work. It also raises crucial questions
with respect to proper and appropriate public perspectives
toward the administrative process in a democratic society.

If, from the point of view of the public, the hallmark of a
democratic election is "competition," it seems appropriate to
designate "balance" as the central concept for the analysis of
the administrative process in a democratic political system.[4]

[3]Herman Finer, "Officials and the Public," *Public Administration*, IX (January
1931), p. 23.
[4]Criteria have been constructed which set forth the conditions under which
election competition is likely to produce a decision based on consent or under
which the competition is likely to degenerate into mass manipulation. See Morris
Janowitz and Dwaine Marvick, *Competitive Pressure and Democratic Consent* (Ann
Arbor: Bur. of Government, Inst. of Public Administration, 1956.)
The following criteria are set forth for judging the quality of an election:
(1) the quality of the election depends on the degree to which competition pro-
duces a high level of citizen participation among all social groups; (2) the quality
of the election depends on the extent to which citizen participation is based on
predispositions of high political self-confidence as well as on self-interest in the
outcome of the elections; (3) the quality of the election depends on the extent
to which competition stimulates effective political deliberation on the issues and
candidates and creates a meaningful basis on which citizens can make their voting
decisions; (4) the quality of the election depends on the extent to which limitations
operate precluding either side from monopolizing or even exercising pervasive
influence by means of the mass media; and (5) the quality of the election depends
on the extent to which the influence of interpersonal pressures operates substantially independent of the influence of the mass media.

Is it possible to give some clarity and precision to the concept of *balance* in analyzing administrative behavior? How can it be used to derive criteria for a model specifying the optimum relations between the bureaucracy and the public? As in the case of the election process, the model is seen as being applicable only to political systems where the essential characteristics of a democratic system are present. Because of the complexities of the administrative process, the only feasible approach seems to describe states of imbalance and to understand balance as some idealized position which avoids or minimizes the disadvantages of different types of imbalance.

A bureaucracy is in imbalance when it fails to operate on the basis of democratic consent:

> Democratic government must provide for all classes a degree of social stability and economic security sufficient to keep these elements loyal to the community of purpose that makes the state possible. Democracy itself will collapse if it creates irreconcilable minorities.[5]

The processes of imbalance are diverse but they can be simply schematized. Bureaucratic imbalance may be either *despotic* or *subservient*. *Despotic* implies that the bureaucracy is too much the master while *subservient* implies that it is too much the servant. The despotic bureaucracy disregards public preference and demands. It is likely to resort to coercion and manipulation to maintain its power. The subservient bureaucracy finds itself so concerned with the demands of special interest groups that it compromises its essential organizational goals and sacrifices essential authority.

Public perspectives toward administrative systems involve basically social relations to symbols of authority. Social science analysis has made considerable progress in demonstrating uniformities in predispositions toward agents and systems of authority. Despite the complexities of administrative systems, perspectives toward them fall into broad categories relevant for describing orientations toward any authority or social system. Three

[5]E. Pendleton Herring, *Public Administration and the Public Interest* (New York: McGraw-Hill, 1936), p. 6.

types of perspectives seem central: *knowledge, self-interest,* and *principle mindedness.* The concept of perspectives rather than attitudes is employed in order to focus on those commitments to action which are directly related to administrative and political decisions. The categories of *knowledge, self-interest,* and *principle mindedness* are defined and elaborated from this point of view.[6]

By *knowledge* we mean a person's level of information. What does a person know about a particular agency or administrative system? Is he poorly or well informed? *Self-interest* is the political measure of gratification. Does the person see administrative authority as serving his self-interest and meeting his essential needs? How does he characterize the performance of administrative agencies? *Principle mindedness* is the moral evaluation of administrative authority. Does the person see the public bureaucracy and the civil servant operating according to a set of accepted and recognized principles and rules of behavior? To these three concepts, it seemed appropriate to add a fourth, *prestige,* which serves as a summary concept and describes public respect or esteem for bureaucracy and the civil servant.

These concepts imply four criteria which help to establish whether, in a specific situation, perspectives toward the public bureaucracy are conducive to administration based on consent, or whether perspectives are conducive to despotic or subservient imbalance. In brief and without justification at this point, the criteria are:

1. *Knowledge.* The public must have an adequate level of knowledge about the operations of the public bureaucracy. Inadequate knowledge facilitates despotic administration, whereas too much knowledge theoretically could deprive an administrative agency of essential autonomy and produce subservient behavior.

2. *Self-interest.* The public must consider that its self-interest is being

---

[6]See Talcott Parsons, *The Social System* (Glencoe, Ill.: Free Press, 1951) for a full elaboration of this problem of orientations towards action. Parsons' categories seem equivalent to those we constructed: knowledge equates to cognition, self-interest to gratification, and principle mindedness to moral evaluation.

served by the public bureaucracy. As a check on the disruptive consequences of self-interested demands on the bureaucracy, the public must be aware simultaneously of the bureaucracy's capacity to act as a neutral and impartial agent in resolving social conflicts.

3. *Principle Mindedness.* The public must be of the general opinion that the public bureaucracy is guided in its actions by a set of principles guaranteeing equal and impersonal treatment. Administrative routines, however, must be sufficiently flexible to cope with individual differences in order to insure adequate dealings with clients.

4. *Prestige.* Public perspective toward the public bureaucracy must include adequate prestige value toward public employment as compared with other types of careers. Very low and very high prestige values would interfere with the bureaucracy's ability to operate on the basis of democratic consent. A very low prestige could tend to bring about subservient administration, while extremely high prestige could tend to result in despotic administration.

Implicit in each of these criteria is a dilemma, or a set of contradictory tendencies, which requires continuous adjustment. The task for the political scientist is to clarify what constitutes the necessary and possible in a democratic society.

Implicit for each criterion is the assumption that it points to a researchable problem. Current methodology is capable of measuring public perspectives and identifying some of the crucial variables which account for them. Thus, this study represents an attempt to apply these criteria empirically.

As a final step in the study, it seemed important to reverse our approach and to investigate what the public officials knew about their clients and the public at large. With what perspectives about clients and the public did the metropolitan-based public officials operate? It seemed necessary also to probe the contacts and channels that public officials had for communicating with their clients. In no sense was there any expectation that such data would answer questions about the specific impact of these forms of communication. Rather, if communications processes involve two-way interaction, such information seems required for an understanding of the limitations and potentials of communications between the public and the bureaucrat.

THE RESEARCH SETTING: THE DETROIT METROPOLITAN COMMUNITY

Public perspectives toward the administrative process were investigated in a metropolitan community setting. The metropolitan community is a territorially localized social system within which the bulk of the daily transactions required for the sustenance of its members takes place.[7] For empirical purposes, the standard metropolitan area of the U.S. Census Bureau defined the limits of the metropolitan community.[8]

Within the metropolitan community all levels of government operate—municipal, county, state, and national. It is a social unit of crucial importance to the student and the practitioner of public administration. Within its borders the role of the administrative process is basic in mediating many sectors of social conflict. When so defined, the metropolitan community constitutes a wide enough network of administrative systems to make empirical research worthwhile, yet manageable in scope.

The objectives of our research were highly exploratory since there were literally no studies of a systematic character which explored public attitudes toward the administrative process. A few studies were available which described attitudes toward specific agencies or toward specific programs.[9] Even the Hadley Cantril compendium of public opinion polling contains very little descriptive attitude data toward public administration.[10] Only the pioneer study of Professor L. D. White on the prestige value of public employment approached the arena of administration in broad conceptual terms.[11]

[7]Amos Hawley, *Human Ecology* (New York: Ronald Press, 1950), pp. 257-58.

[8]A standard metropolitan area is a county, or group of contiguous counties, which contains at least one city of 50,000 inhabitants or more. In addition to the county or counties containing such a city, contiguous counties are included in a standard metropolitan area if, according to certain criteria, they are essentially metropolitan in character and are socially and economically integrated with the central city.

[9]G. Douglas Gourley, *Public Relations and the Police* (Springfield, Ill.: Thornes, 1953). Also, *Public Relations of Public Personnel Agencies* (Chicago: Civil Service Assembly, 1941).

[10]Hadley Cantril, *Public Opinion, 1935–46* (Princeton: Princeton Univ. Press, 1951).

[11]Leonard D. White, *The Prestige Value of Public Employment* (Chicago: Univ. of Chicago Press, 1929). Also, Leonard D. White, *Further Contributions to the Prestige Value of Public Employment* (Chicago: Univ. of Chicago Press, 1932).

The Detroit metropolitan community was used as our research site. The empirical data which constitute the basis of this analysis were gathered in February 1954 from a representative sample survey of 764 abults in the Detroit metropolitan area, through the facilities of the Detroit Area Study of the University of Michigan.[12] Each year the Detroit Area Study, operating with an area probability sample, conducts a sample survey of the Detroit metropolitan community as part of the advanced training and research program of the social sciences at the University of Michigan. Most interviews were between one and one and a half hours in length.

Besides the interviews with the cross section of the adult population, a questionnaire was administered to a specialized sample of upper and lower level public officials in three key integrative (service) agencies: the Bureau of Old Age and Survivors Insurance, the Michigan Employment Security Commission, and the Detroit Board of Education. This questionnaire was designed to collect the required data on their level of knowledge and their perspectives concerning clients and the public at large. It was also designed to describe patterns of contact and communication between public officials and their various publics.

Undoubtedly, local political and administrative conditions in Detroit conditioned the population's perspectives toward the public bureaucracy. Detroit, like each of the major metropolitan areas, has special industrial features. It has, for example, a

[12]The area covered by the Detroit Area Study does not coincide exactly with the official Detroit Standard Metropolitan Area of the U. S. Census Bureau, which includes all of Wayne, Macomb, and Oakland counties. The Detroit Area Study excludes those outlying sectors of the three counties which are not divided into census tracts. The region covered by its sample includes approximately 89 per cent of the population of the three counties. Approximately 2/3 of the interviews were taken in the city of Detroit; 1/3 were taken outside of Detroit in the cities, villages and unincorporated parts of the suburban area. Since the survey was restricted to private dwelling units, those people residing in military establishments, hospitals, religious and educational institutions, transient hotels, and large rooming houses were excluded from the sample. Those excluded probably comprise less than 5 per cent of the adult population of Detroit. By means of repeated calls back, interviews were completed in 86 per cent of the homes on the original interview list. See Appendix A, Sampling Technique.

particularly high concentration of recent southern migrants. Nevertheless, since the majority of the United States population resides in such metropolitan areas and since there is no reason to believe that Detroit is unique, these empirical findings have relatively broad relevance.

More crucial than the special social characteristics of the Detroit area are the general consequences of studying public perspectives toward the administrative process at the metropolitan community level. The advantages that accrue from working in a research site that is complex yet manageable must be weighed against the range of administrative decisions that had to be deliberately eliminated. It was appropriate to focus on those functions of governmental administration which directly regulate and pervade the daily existence of the population of the metropolitan community. Our working definition of the metropolitan community required such a focus. This meant that agencies conducting foreign affairs and remote aspects of national politics and economic policy would not be stressed, even though in the long run, these are crucial to the very existence of the metropolitan community. Some agencies whose ultimate objectives were more broadly national or international in scope, however, were included because their functions directly impinged on residents in a metropolitan community. For example, the selective service was included in our study.

An administrative agency was defined as a formally organized bureaucracy which serves to implement the legislative and judicial decisions made by any level of government. Given this definition, the most crucial and difficult problem was to sample the agencies of the public bureaucracy. On what basis could a limited number of agencies be selected for investigation which would be "representative," in a meaningful sense, of the spectrum of agencies which affect the daily life of the average citizen. Three points can be made.

1. The selection of an agency did not imply that it had to have its entire basis of operations in the Detroit metropolitan community. Rather, the agency had to have personnel and functions located in the metropolitan community.

2. It was necessary to concentrate on agencies with relatively high visibility and relatively direct contact with the public.

3. All of the agencies selected affected significant aspects of the behavior of the population of the metropolitan community. Efforts to select only the most important ones seemed impossible. Nor was any statistical representation possible. Instead, the selection was related to the model of balance in administrative behavior. All levels of government were included and selected agencies reflected the broad range of governmental activities.[13]

The list of agencies involved in the interview included: *federal*, Bureau of Old Age and Survivors Insurance, Selective Service System, and Bureau of Internal Revevue; *state*, Michigan Employment Security Commission, and state police; *local*, public school system, public library, public transportation service, street and alley cleaning, municipal police, county police, and tax assessor's office. In addition, general questions were included on municipal, county, and state government. The interview objective was to chart patterns of contact with these administrative agencies and to record levels of knowledge and evaluation of public administration. It was also designed to investigate feelings of self-interest and prestige values.

Was it possible, as a result of the interview, to collect the

[13]The formal distinction between integrative functions and allocative functions made for analyzing social institutions and social control supplied an important criterion for selecting administrative agencies. By allocative functions is meant those activities which fix and distribute roles, duties, and responsibilities among members of a community. See Talcott Parsons and Edward Shils, *Toward a General Theory of Action* (Cambridge, Mass.: Harvard Univ. Press, 1952). Allocative functions establish the division of labor. By integrative functions is meant those activities which enable the member of a community to carry out his role, duties, and responsibilities. Integrative functions make possible participation in and continuance of the division of labor. By the interaction of allocative and integrative functions the community is able to function. For example, an agency such as the Selective Service can be considered primarily allocative in that as it determines who shall serve in the armed forces, it establishes roles. By contrast, the Public Health Service has mainly integrative functions in that it assists persons in dealing with the health problems created by urban life. Certain agencies have both integrative and allocative functions, depending on the social groups involved. Moreover, the whole process of administration can be seen in terms of the balance between allocative functions—the obligations exacted—and integrative functions—the services and assistance provided. Therefore, it was necessary to sample both integrative and allocative agencies.

types of data necessary to document these basic perspectives toward symbols of administrative authority? Reactions to authority reveal the core of personality and involve complex reactions. Is the relatively short (one to one and a half hour) open-end interview with standardized probes an effective instrument for describing such attitudes?

In some respects, our approach was effective. The interview was constructed to avoid quizzing the respondent. Instead, the interview was designed to lead the respondent through a discussion of civic problems in the context of community and metropolitan life. We were concerned lest those interviewed would find these matters uninteresting and therefore be difficult to interview. Contrary to our expectation, there was considerable involvement and interest on these presumably unexciting topics. In retrospect the reason becomes obvious, and fortunately our interview approach did not weaken the inherent rapport-building aspects of the subject matter. The activities of administrative agencies, as they were presented in the interview, were viewed essentially as important extensions of family and household concerns. The character of the interview—and all interviews have their own character—pointed in this direction because of the specific questions on neighborhood and community relations that were included. The interest was of the low-pressure variety and conditioned the type of rapport that was created. High-pressure matters such as world communism and foreign affairs had been excluded. The school system, the police, the local government, the state government, social security, and even the selective service were hardly remote, however. Questions about them produced an unselfconscious and relatively free flow of response.

The fact that the interview was based on standardized probing and was limited in duration was an advantage. The hostility that was expressed was manifest hostility of the type that would be directly and more consciously involved in daily perspectives. Undoubtedly more intensive probing would have mobilized greater hostility lodged more deeply in personality structure. But what would such hostility mean for this investigation? Our concern was to chart attitudes of acceptance and rejection of government agencies and to tap underlying consensus as it operates in the daily setting of the metropolitan community. More intensive interviewing is required to probe orientations to the nationalistic symbols that a crisis would mobilize. Therefore, this type of interview, and not a more intensive one, was appropriate for the objectives of this investigation. It made possible a systematic investigation of four concepts—knowledge, self-interest, principle mindedness, and prestige—requisite to a theory of administrative behavior based on consent.

II

LEVEL OF KNOWLEDGE

KNOWLEDGE and information on any political issue imply an underlying interest in that issue. For the public to be fully informed on all political issues is a utopian goal. The public fully informed on all political issues would in fact imply an underlying conflict of interest so pervasive that the possibility of resolving conflicts on the basis of persuasion and negotiation would be low. Likewise, in a modern urban society it is not possible or even desirable to have every citizen well informed about each administrative agency. Theoretically, just as nonvoting can have a positive social function in containing and dampening election conflict, so public indifference can reflect agreement about administrative matters. Such indifference can be a positive contribution to the tasks of the administrative process. Danger arises when indifference is widespread or becomes concentrated in particular social groups.

Moreover, the acquiring of factual knowledge per se may not always rest on motives that are appropriate for a democratic society. In a sense, all decisions must be made with limited knowledge. The "inside dopester," to use David Riesman's phrase,[1] shows a psychological concern with masses of factual detail in order to justify his perpetual claim that no action is possible until more knowledge is accumulated. A balanced public bureaucracy is possible not because knowledge can be amassed but rather because knowledge is utilized as a basis of judgment and action. The sabotage of administration by the full search for the facts and by the full compliance with the letter of the law is well known. If the population were composed exclusively of graduates of public administration and law schools, government action might well come to a halt!

In his *Torment of Secrecy*, Edward A. Shils calls for a balance between "publicity, privacy, and secrecy" in order to meet the requirements of security policies in a democratic and pluralistic

[1]David Riesman, *Faces in the Crowd* (New Haven: Yale Univ. Press, 1952).

society.[2] Clearly, the concept of privacy applies to all administrators and administrative agencies—sensitive or not—since reflection, discretion, and administrative leadership are impossible without some measure of privacy. Privacy implies a degree of public ignorance and a willingness on the part of the public and the press to accept the need for some administrative privacy. Although theoretically too much public knowledge could unbalance the effectiveness of a particular bureaucracy, clearly the issue in the urban metropolitan community is the lack of adequate knowledge. On what basis, therefore, is it possible to determine what is an adequate level of knowledge?

It cannot be argued that the public can remain ignorant of the processes of government, as long as it has a favorable framework of attitudes toward basic agencies and services. Such a point of view overlooks the fact that favorable attitudes towards governmental agencies must be rooted in and are likely to develop out of factual knowledge. Moreover, factual knowledge is required to give the public some reasonable picture of what it can expect from governmental services—to give the citizen a time perspective on the future.

We sought, therefore, to develop an approach to the level of public information based on a sampling of some crucial areas of administrative behavior. Granted that an individual would specialize his knowledge in terms of his self-interest, there must also be areas of self-interest common to the members of the metropolitan community in general. Clearly we were not interested in any specific areas per se, and the ones chosen constituted no more than an index. Other questions could be substituted, but we assumed that the over-all distribution of results—the encountered levels of knowledge—would not be altered. For the specialist to object to a specific item is somewhat irrelevant. The basic goal was to construct an over-all test applicable to the public at large and designed to distinguish between the better informed and the less informed. The validity of the approach is inferred in part from the results which indicate that levels

[2]Edward A. Shils, *The Torment of Secrecy* (Glencoe, Ill.: Free Press, 1956).

of knowledge about governmental administration are not the same as an individual's educational attainment, which is rooted in other social factors.

For example, in insisting that the bulk of the population ought to have "adequate" knowledge of the important public welfare programs, it is hardly suggested that the details of eligibility requirements and benefits must be known. But, if people lack elementary knowledge of their status under these programs and the major risks which are covered, the objectives of the programs are frustrated and the daily tasks of the administrator are immensely complicated. In terms of our model, if lack of knowledge is widespread or if lack of knowledge is especially concentrated in some particular social grouping, then the public bureaucracy will tend to act without balance.

On the basis of these considerations, it was possible to determine the extent to which public perspectives in the Detroit metropolitan community conformed to or deviated from our first basic criterion concerning public knowledge:

The public must have an adequate level of knowledge about the operations of the public bureaucracy. Inadequate knowledge facilitates despotic administration, whereas too much knowledge theoretically could deprive an administrative agency of essential autonomy and produce subservient behavior.

GENERALIZED VERSUS INSTRUMENTAL KNOWLEDGE

To clarify this criterion concerning adequate knowledge of the public bureaucracy, it seemed appropriate to make a distinction between generalized knowledge and instrumental knowledge.[3] Instrumental knowledge is crucial information about the immediate consequences of administration as they impinge on an individual; it is information, essential to an individual, about

[3]This distinction relates to the theoretical analysis of Karl Mannheim in *Ideology and Utopia*, where he speaks of substantive rationality and functional rationality. Functional rationality, for Mannheim, was understanding of the immediate workings of a social situation or institution; that is, *means* oriented knowledge. Substantive rationality refers to wider understanding of the interrelations of various social situations and institutions; that is, *ends* oriented knowledge. See Karl Mannheim, *Ideology and Utopia* (New York: Harcourt Brace, 1936).

his rights and obligations with respect to a specific agency. Generalized knowledge deals with the over-all working of the agency and the system of administration. Generalized knowledge indicates a level of awareness of the system and how it operates. The distinction, of course, is a matter of degree. For example, to know that the office of police commissioner is an appointive post and not an elective one is generalized knowledge about the police department. To know of the existence of a complaint bureau in the police department and to know how to make use of it is instrumental knowledge.

By investigating a series of simple but central factual questions about public administration, it was possible to ascertain the level of a person's generalized knowledge and to test the hypothesis that the level of generalized knowledge was a function of position in the social structure. It must be stressed that the factual knowledge required to "pass" was indeed simple. Moreover, the items are not crucial per se but merely represent a selection used to differentiate the persons interviewed. Typical of the range levels of correct generalized knowledge were the following:

Thirteen per cent knew about what portion of the national budget was spent on national defense and foreign aid.

Twenty-eight per cent knew that the Board of Education was made up of elected officials.

Fifty-six per cent knew the amount at which income taxes started and income tax returns had to be filed.[4]

The level of generalized knowledge, of course, is determined by the specific questions asked. We expected that correct responses would be low and in fact they were low. But since we did not make use of the ideal model of the fully informed citizen, it was difficult to draw the conclusion that these levels

[4]The text of the questions were:

1. Of all the taxes paid to the government in Washington, what portion would you say is being used to pay for national defense and foreign aid? 2/3 or more; about 1/2; 1/3 or less.

2. Do you happen to know how the people on the Board of Education get their jobs?

3. Do you happen to know how much money a person had to make last year before he had to file an income tax return this March 15?

were dangerously low for a system of public administration based on democratic consent. For these data to assume full meaning, comparative trend data involving earlier time periods and other democratic political systems are required. Such data we do not have.

Nor were cumulative scores particularly clarifying. The cumulative scores of generalized knowledge, as was expected, were positively related to social class and to education (Table I).[5] The association of generalized knowledge with educational level is statistically significant as between the extreme groups

TABLE I

SOCIAL GROUP DIFFERENCES IN LEVEL OF GENERALIZED KNOWLEDGE
(In per cent)

Social Characteristics	Level of Generalized Knowledge					Number of Cases
	Low*	Middle†	High‡	Not Ascertained	Total	
Social Class						
Lower Lower ..	22	42	29	7	100	(250)
Upper Lower ..	22	45	25	8	100	(207)
Lower Middle..	17	36	37	10	100	(186)
Upper Middle..	14	35	46	5	100	(106)
Education						
Less then elementary ..	29	31	18	22	100	(133)
Elementary	22	46	25	7	100	(105)
Some high school	22	42	31	5	100	(173)
High school	18	42	36	4	100	(236)
Some or completed college.	7	39	53	1	100	(109)
Negro–White						
White	20	39	33	8	100	(658)
Negro	23	44	24	9	100	(106)
Sex						
Male	18	40	36	6	100	(360)
Female	22	40	29	9	100	(404)

*Answered none of the three questions on generalized knowledge correctly.
†Answered one of the three questions on generalized knowledge correctly.
‡Answered two or three of the three questions on generalized knowledge correctly.

[5]See Appendix D for the operationalization of social class.

with the least and with the most education.[6] No doubt increased education will raise the level of generalized knowledge. But civic education in the metropolitan community has clear limitations. The link between education and generalized knowledge was hardly so pronounced, and the level attained even by the college-educated hardly so high, as to expect the present and future performance of educational institutions to produce automatic solutions. Only about half (53 per cent) of those who attended or completed college answered more than one of the generalized knowledge questions correctly. (From Table I it can be seen that whites were somewhat better informed than Negroes, and men slightly better informed than women. Undoubtedly the level of education was at work here.)

Instrumental knowledge was thought to be a more relevant basis for applying and evaluating the first basic precondition for a public bureaucracy in a democratic setting. By selecting key aspects of administrative programs at the metropolitan community level, the public could be judged as to whether it possessed essential knowledge of these programs.

For three agencies, which penetrate the metropolitan community on a mass basis, the level of instrumental knowledge displayed must also be considered low from any standpoint:

Twenty-two per cent knew the length of coverage under unemployment insurance.

Twenty-six per cent knew of both major types of protection—old-age and survivors insurance—under the social security system.

Fifty-six per cent were aware in the most general terms of an appeal procedure under the selective service system.[7]

When cumulative scores on instrumental knowledge were classified by social group characteristics, the group differences

[6]Tests of statistical significance were employed to determine whether the observed differences were due to sampling (chance) error or to actual differences between groups. Throughout the text, where a significant difference is reported, it is at least at the .05 confidence limit.

[7]The text of the questions were:

1. Do you know how many weekly checks a person can get under unemployment insurance?

2. What benefits does social security entitle you to?

3. If someone isn't satisfied with how the draft board has classified him, could he try to change it? What could he do?

paralleled those at work for generalized knowledge (Table II). Higher social class position and better education were linked to a higher level of instrumental knowledge. Negroes and women appeared relatively worse off on this type of knowledge. In fact, social group differences on instrumental knowledge were somewhat sharper than in the case of generalized knowledge.

SOCIAL WELFARE: A TEST CASE

Since the social security system is an integrative (service) agency with extremely wide impact, it was appropriate as a case study to investigate the level of knowledge about this

TABLE II

SOCIAL GROUP DIFFERENCES IN LEVEL OF INSTRUMENTAL KNOWLEDGE
(In per cent)

Social Characteristics	Level of Instrumental Knowledge					
	Low*	Middle†	High‡	Not Ascertained	Total	Number of Cases
Social Class						
Lower Lower...	15	38	41	6	100	(250)
Upper Lower...	15	28	51	6	100	(207)
Lower Middle..	11	27	53	9	100	(186)
Upper Middle ..	3	24	66	7	100	(106)
Education						
Less than elementary ..	32	27	30	11	100	(133)
Elementary	14	36	43	7	100	(105)
Some high school	13	36	46	4	100	(173)
High school	6	30	55	9	100	(236)
Some or completed college.	6	23	68	3	100	(109)
Negro–White						
White	11	30	52	7	100	(658)
Negro	22	35	37	6	100	(106)
Sex						
Male	7	26	59	8	100	(360)
Female	19	34	40	7	100	(404)

*Answered none of the three questions on instrumental knowledge correctly.
†Answered one of the three questions on instrumental knowledge correctly.
‡Answered two or three of the three questions on instrumental knowledge correctly.

agency in greater detail.[8] In particular, two sets of factors—position in the social structure and social welfare experiences—seemed important to investigate as conditioning the level of instrumental knowledge. First, how did a person's educational background and his position in the social structure relate to his instrumental knowledge of social security benefits? Second, how did his actual contact—personal and familial—with the social security program influence his instrumental knowledge?

The fullest generalized understanding of the processes of government would reside in the better educated groups and in the middle and upper social classes. Nevertheless, it was an underlying hypothesis that educational attainment and corresponding position in the social structure would not adequately account for what people knew about benefit rights under social security or any other integrative agency. Instrumental knowledge about the processes of government, we anticipated, would also be conditioned by program and agency contact. Since these programs cut across the class lines (and therefore educational levels), their actual impact—direct and indirect—ought to disseminate functional knowledge into the lower classes. In other terms, the self-interest of the public and its actual contact with these integrative programs were expected to work in the direction of overcoming educational limitations.

Thus, with respect to instrumental knowledge about social security benefits, we found that in addition to 26 per cent with correct knowledge about social security benefits, 48 per cent gave partially correct answers, 12 per cent gave incorrect answers, while 14 per cent were in the "don't know" or "not ascertained" category.

As a result of the simple way in which questions were posed and the answers scored, the low figure of 26 per cent with correct knowledge about social security benefits tends to err, if it errs at all, in favor of overestimating the percentage of correct answers.[9] A correct answer meant awareness that social

[8]See Morris Janowitz, "Public Perspectives on Social Security," *Social Work*, I (July 1956), pp. 94-101.

[9]The text of the question was: What benefits does social security entitle you to? Responses or lack of responses were followed up by standardized probing.

security provided both old-age and survivors benefits. The 48 per cent who had partially correct answers consisted of those who mentioned only old-age benefits (45 per cent) and the very small percentage (3 per cent) who cited survivors' benefits only. Since the partially correct answer generally meant failure to include survivors' benefits, it is indeed striking to note the extent to which the respondents, even after probing, were unaware of this crucial social welfare benefit. In addition, 21 per cent of the persons interviewed gave answers which can only be interpreted as reflecting incorrect, inadequate, or just no knowledge of social security benefits.

The link between formal education and level of instrumental knowledge about social security benefits was found to be statistically present (Table III). It is, however, a relationship

TABLE III

INSTRUMENTAL KNOWLEDGE OF SOCIAL SECURITY BENEFITS, EDUCATION, AND SOCIAL CLASS

(In per cent)

Knowledge of Benefits	Education				
	Some Elementary	Completed Elementary	Some High School	Graduated High School	College
Correct	11	14	25	31	45
Partially correct..	50	52	53	46	44
Incorrect	13	19	12	13	6
Don't know; not ascertained	26	15	10	10	5
	100	100	100	100	100
Number of cases	(113)	(133)	(173)	(236)	(109)

Knowledge of Benefits	Social Class			
	Lower Working	Upper Working	Lower Middle	Upper Middle
Correct	20	22	28	45
Partially	49	52	49	40
Incorrect	20	12	8	5
Don't know; not ascertained	11	14	15	10
	100	100	100	100
Number of cases .	(250)	(207)	(186)	(106)

that is mainly for those with very high education or with very limited education—the extremes, so to speak. But even the college-educated hardly presented a really "passing" grade. Of those with college education 45 per cent gave correct responses, while of those with some elementary education only 8 per cent gave correct answers. The pattern of correct knowledge varied much less for the groups with more average amounts of education. Furthermore, the consequence of education factor was most important for correct answers only. Partially correct answers were spread through the population almost without regard to level of education.

Likewise, when the link between social class position and level of instrumental knowledge was investigated, an increasing level of correct knowledge about social security was encountered for each higher social class position (Table III). The next step in the analysis, therefore, was to examine directly how far agency contact conditioned level of knowledge.

In analyzing the impact of agency contact with the social security program, it was first necessary to ascertain who had dealings with the program aside from making contributions. What were the social class backgrounds of those who had such contacts? Contact with social security meant that the individual respondent was a member of a family, at least one member of which was receiving benefits: either old-age benefits or survivors' benefits or both.

The social security program was originally expected to have a special impact on the working class. Nevertheless, social security has had a history of gradual extension of coverage.[10] As a result, the social class backgrounds of those who have received benefits reveal the striking extent to which this program cuts across social class lines.

As of the time of the survey, 20 per cent of the sample reported that they were members of families in which at least one person was receiving old-age or survivors' benefits, or both.

[10]"The Social Security Act: The First Twenty Years," *Social Security Bulletin* (August 1955). See especially Wilbur J. Cohen, "*Social Security Objectives and Achievement*," pp. 2-5.

The finding that an almost similar percentage of families in both the working and middle classes were currently receiving social security benefits was unexpected and highlights the extent to which this program has already been functioning for the community at large (Table IV).

Approximately 18 per cent of each of the upper working class, the lower middle class, and the upper middle class reported that some member of their family was receiving social security benefits. Nor was there any difference for these class groups as to type of benefit. Only for the lower working class was the percentage somewhat higher (25 per cent) and this probably included some recipients of direct old-age assistance.

Examination of the consequences of agency contact of all social groups, however, brings into sharp relief the strategic problem of developing a democratically informed public. It was not surprising that, for each of the specific social class groupings, contact (personal and family) improved knowledge of benefits of both programs (Table V). What is crucial is that the pragmatic education provided by contact with these agencies eliminated the disabilities derived from a lack of formal education among those in low social class positions.

TABLE IV

MEMBER OF RESPONDENT'S FAMILY RECEIVING SOCIAL SECURITY
AND SOCIAL CLASS OF RESPONDENT

(In per cent)

Benefit Status	Social Class				
	Lower Working	Upper Working	Lower Middle	Upper Middle	Total*
Receives some type of benefit	25	18	17	18	20
Receives no benefit ...	71	75	75	75	74
Not ascertained; don't know	4	7	8	7	6
	100	100	100	100	100
Number of cases	(250)	(207)	(186)	(106)	(764)

*Total column includes 15 cases for which social class breakdown could not be ascertained.

TABLE V

Knowledge of Social Security Benefits and Family Unit Receipt of Benefits, Shown by Social Class

(In per cent)

Knowledge of Benefits	Social Class of Family Unit							
	Lower Working		Upper Working		Lower Middle		Upper Middle	
	Benefits rec'd*	No benefits	Benefits rec'd*	No benefits	Benefits rec'd*	No benefits	Benefits rec'd*	No benefits
Correct	40	15	34	20	24	29	66	39
Partially correct	48	50	58	50	73	45	29	43
Incorrect	10	23	3	14	3	8	5	5
Don't know; not ascertained	2	12	5	16	..	18	..	13
	100	100	100	100	100	100	100	100
Number of Cases.........	(52)	(198)	(38)	(169)	(29)	(157)	(21)	(85)

*Respondent was a member of a family unit in which at least one person was receiving old-age or survivors' benefits, or both.

Forty per cent of the lower working class who had had contact gave correct answers to the queries about social security benefits, a proportion which exceeded both the upper working class and the lower middle class.[11] In fact, there appears a tendency for less knowledge to be derived from contact as one moves up the social class ladder, with the marked exception of the upper middle class. Here is direct evidence that the lower classes are not disproportionately uninformed as to their stake in the social security program; self-interest operates to overcome educational limitations. Nevertheless, it is necessary to keep in mind that the amount of ignorance which persisted in all classes even after personal and family contact with this basic social welfare program is indeed immense. This is not merely the case for the administration of social security. The same state of affairs exists for unemployment compensation and other integrative aspects of administration in the metropolitan community. Thus, because of the level of ignorance that persists even after personal and family contact with administrative agencies, the first criterion for administration based on consent—the requirement of adequate information—is not fully satisfied.

These low levels of public information—generalized and instrumental—need to be evaluated in the context of the public's approval of the objectives of metropolitan-based administration. Lack of knowledge did not result from indifference or lack of approval of the performance of metropolitan administration. Here the social welfare agencies are a revealing case in point. For example, as of 1955, the idea of "social security" was so well accepted that in our pretesting, it was impossible to find any statistically meaningful group which was opposed to the underlying principle. Also, only 6 per cent of our Detroit sample thought unemployment insurance was bad for the country. We are, however, anticipating the application of the

[11]In the case of lower middle class, increased knowledge about social security benefits through contact presents a somewhat different pattern. There is a slight, but statistically not significant, decrease in correct knowledge as contact increases and a very marked increase in partially correct knowledge.

second basic criterion—that of self-interest—namely the extent to which the public accepts the performance of the public bureaucracy as serving its self-interest.

III

THE WORTH OF GOVERNMENT: SELF-INTEREST REDEFINED

A PUBLIC bureaucracy which the individual does not see as serving utilitarian goals must of necessity rely on despotic practices to preserve its authority and power. In the language of political theory, the political consequences of each person pursuing his self-interest serve to counterbalance bureaucratic abuse. But political theory, likewise, has long recognized that self-interest alone is clearly not a sufficient basis for insuring social order. Although individual self-interest is a basis for organizing a democratic political system, the blind pursuit of self-interest can wreck a political system. Political theorists have therefore come to speak of enlightened self-interest, as opposed to blind self-interest. Enlightened self-interest implies a willingness to balance off immediate self-interest goals against broader goals generated by membership in the larger political system.

This implies that each person must see the administrative system as capable of maintaining a balance between serving his self-interests and operating to resolve conflicting social interests. In other terms, self-interest relevant for democratic consent means that the individual recognizes that the government not only operates to "integrate" him into the metropolitan community, but the government must also "allocate" responsibilities and burdens.[1] These considerations lead to the formulation of our second criterion of administration based on consent:

For administrative behavior to be based on democratic consent, the public must consider that its self-interest is being served by the public bureaucracy. As a check on the disruptive consequences of self-interested demands on the bureaucracy, the public must simultaneously be aware of the bureaucracy's capacity to act as a neutral and impartial agent in solving social conflicts.

At least three different dimensions seem to be implied in this criterion of redefined self-interest. Our methodology seemed

[1]See Robert A. Dahl and Charles E. Lindblom, *Politics, Economics and Welfare*, (New York: Harpers, 1953), especially Chapter II, for a discussion of this problem.

adequate to investigate the extent to which the public held attitudes compatible with each of these three dimensions.

First, self-interest, as redefined, could only be operative if the public's estimate of the current performance of administrative agencies was basically favorable. Democratic elections function because both sides limit the struggle and basically accept the electoral institutions. Likewise, fundamental acceptance of the performance of the administrative process is required for public administration to operate on the basis of consent. Criticism must take place within fundamental acceptance of administrative authority. Therefore, we had to investigate the extent to which such acceptance and consensus existed. This we called the performance *acceptance-rejection* dimension.

Second, in a democratic society, self-interest, as redefined, must involve an important element of agreement about the goals and scope of administrative behavior. In the metropolitan setting, it was appropriate to investigate this dimension in terms of the welfare function of government. To what extent was there agreement about the goals and scope of the public bureaucracy in this area? This we called the *scope of government* dimension.

Third, it was necessary to explore a person's estimate of the worth of government services. Self-interest, redefined, meant that an individual would feel that the "costs" of government are worthwhile because of the benefits that derive from governmental administration. In the marked absence of such a belief, self-interest could hardly be operative and therefore we had to investigate the extent of this particular perspective. This we called the *worth of government* dimension. In each of these three dimensions we were interested less in perspectives toward specific agencies, per se, and more in seeking to describe general attitudes toward the administrative process at the metropolitan community level.

Acceptance-Rejection

The acceptance-rejection dimension was investigated by means of a quantitative scale. Since perspectives toward administrative agencies may be viewed as orientations toward symbols of authority, it was assumed that a person's acceptance-rejection of different administrative agencies would not be just accidental and diffuse. Rather, it was assumed that a person's evaluation of the performance of administrative agencies would fall into a relatively uniform pattern. Individual judgments of different agencies would be inter-related; there would be some essential unity to the way he viewed the various agencies that operated in the metropolitan community. Administration at the level of the metropolitan community—regardless of governmental level—impinges on the individual as a system of authority and control. This did not mean that a person would be uniform in his evaluation of the performance of specific agencies, always accepting or always rejecting. It was expected that a person's estimate of the specific agencies would vary but that, if he had a tendency to reject some administrative authorities, this tendency would condition his evaluation of other authorities. Likewise, the perspective he manifested toward specific agencies would tend to coincide with his over-all evaluation of administrative systems. Thus, in the language of quantitative research, attitudes of acceptance and rejection of different administrative authorities would be scalable.

Only a minimum test was undertaken to determine whether acceptance-rejection attitudes toward administrative performance were scalable or fell into a uniform pattern.[2] Respondents were not presented with a long list of agencies and asked to check acceptance or rejection. Such a mechanical approach could produce statistically uniform results but would not necessarily test the assumption in a realistic and meaningful context. Instead, those metropolitan-based agencies or administrative

[2]The Guttman scaling technique was employed. See Samuel A. Stouffer and others, *Measurement and Prediction*, Vol. IV, in *Studies in Social Psychology in World War II* (Princeton: Princeton Univ. Press, 1950).

systems chosen to be investigated had to be of a highly visible nature. Moreover, both regulative and integrative (service) agencies had to be included in the scale.

The findings of the Detroit Area Study support the assumption that this acceptance-rejection dimension does fall into a generalized pattern. Five crucial agencies and administrative groupings selected in terms of the above criteria produced a Guttman-type scale meeting the statistical requirements of scalability (Table VI).[3] The scale included public perspectives toward the local schools, local officials and bureaus, state officials and bureaus, local police, and state police. How an individual feels about a particular agency is, then, a crucial indicator as to how he feels about other administrative agencies and, by implication, about the administrative system in general.

The fact that these data were so structured meant that, within the context of the metropolitan community, we could speak with some assurance about a generalized perspective toward the public bureaucracy on the basis of administrative performance. In short, this crucial syndrome did in fact exist.

The basic public acceptance of the performance of metropolitan community based agencies can be seen in the relatively low percentages of outspokenly critical responses that emerged on this acceptance-rejection scale. Only 9 per cent of the sample rejected or were hostile to the performance of all five of the administrative authorities (scale type six). Another 7 per cent reacted negatively to four out of the five administrative authorities (scale type five). Perhaps more meaningful measures were the component attitudes of this scale, namely the level of extreme criticism expressed against particular agencies. Outspokenly critical evaluations ranged from 16 per cent who rated the public school system *very unfavorable* to only 2 per cent who evaluated the state police *very unfavorable*:

	Outspokenly Critical
Administrative Authority	*Evaluations*
Public Schools	
Quest: "How do you feel about the public schools in (community name)?"	16%

[3]The reproducibility of the scale was .924.

Administrative Authority	Outspokenly Critical Evaluations
Local Officials and Bureaus	
Quest: "Do you think (community name) officials and bureaus are doing a poor, fair, good, or very good job?"	6%
State Officials and Bureaus	
Quest: "And the state government—do you think the state officials and bureaus are doing a poor, fair, good, or very good job?"	4%
Local Police	
Quest: "What kind of a job would you say the (community name) police are doing?" ...	6%
State Police	
Quest: "And the State Police—how good a job are they doing?	2%

These attitudes on current performance are, of course, no measure of demands for improvement, a subject which was not investigated.

A slightly wider range of critically negative opinion of performance was found among a separate group of local government agencies, judgments of which were asked only of persons who had had contact with the particular agency during the past year. For these agencies—the public library, the tax assessor, the street and alley cleaning division, and the public transportation system—contact was considered a prerequisite for asking opinions on performance. In the case of the public library, there was no outspoken criticism at all among the 33 per cent of the sample having had contact. By contrast, the public transportation system produced 24 per cent critical responses among the 64 per cent who had made use of it.[4] No doubt the purely local character of these agencies as well

[4]The range of contact and evaluation for these four agencies was:

	Contact during Last Year	Outspokenly Critical Evaluation*
Public Library	33%	—
Tax Assessor	30%	2%
Street and Alley Cleaning	42%	10%
Public Transportation	64%	24%

*Only of those who had contact.

TABLE VI

SCALABILITY OF PUBLIC PERSPECTIVE TOWARD PERFORMANCE OF ADMINISTRATIVE AUTHORITIES

(ACCEPTANCE–REJECTION DIMENSION)

Plus equals favorable evaluation of performance (acceptance).
Minus equals unfavorable evaluation of performance (rejection).

Scale Types	State Police	Local Police	State Officials and Bureaus	Local Officials and Bureaus	Schools	Number of Cases	Percentage
One (acceptance)	Plus	Plus	Plus	Plus	Plus	(121)	16
Two	Plus	Plus	Plus	Plus	Minus	(163)	21
Three	Plus	Plus	Plus	Minus	Minus	(142)	19
Four	Plus	Plus	Minus	Minus	Minus	(119)	16
Five	Plus	Minus	Minus	Minus	Minus	(58)	7
Six (rejection)	Minus	Minus	Minus	Minus	Minus	(70)	9
Don't know						(44)	6
Not ascertained						(47)	6
Total						(764)	100

as the greater familiarity tended to produce this range of critical response. Nevertheless, the percentages are hardly extreme and do not overshadow the basic acceptance of the current performance of the metropolitan bureaucracy.

The Scope of Government

The second dimension of self-interest—the scope of government—was measured by means of the following question:

Some people think the national government should do more in trying to deal with such problems as unemployment, education, housing, and so on. Others think that the government is already doing too much. On the whole, would you say that what the government has done has been about right, too much, or not enough?

It should be noted that only 7 per cent of the Detroit metropolitan community sample believed that the public bureaucracy was doing too much in these areas (Table VII). These responses, in particular, indicate the degree to which public attitudes apparently diverge from those manifested by the typical contents of the mass media and the rhetoric of political debate. Thwarted self-interest and anti-government attitudes are hardly the dominant themes. Forty-six per cent thought that the present scope was about right or were pro-con; 40 per cent said it was not enough while 7 per cent expressed no opinion or were not ascertainable. This latter figure is indeed a very low percentage and runs counter to the assumption of the unstructuredness of opinions on crucial political matters. Overwhelmingly, the issue is between the desire to maintain the status quo and the pressure for the expansion of governmental activities.

As expected, the demands for expansion were concentrated in the lower social class groupings (see Table VIII). Except for the proportion in the upper middle class who felt that the public bureaucracy was too active in these areas (16 per cent), the social class differences do not seem to present profound political cleavages.

To a greater extent, the responses revealed a difference between the Negro and the white population, with the low

TABLE VII

Perspectives Toward the Public Bureaucracy

Scope of Government

Some people think the national government should do more in trying to deal with such problems as unemployment, education, housing, and so on. Others think that the government is already doing too much. On the whole, would you say that what the government has done has been about right, too much, or not enough?

Too Much	About right; pro-con	Not enough	Don't know; Not ascertained	Number of Cases
7%	46%	40%	7%	(764)

Worth of Government Services

As some people see it, there are different kinds of things the government has to do. The government has to provide help for people. The government also has to make people carry their share of the burdens and make sacrifices. Which of these statements comes closest to your own opinion about this?

(a) The help and services that the public gets from the government is worth what it asks from the public.

(b) The government asks more from the public than it gives in help and services.

(c) The public gets more from the government than it gives the government.

Government asks more	Government services are worth burden	Public gets more	Don't know; not ascertained	Number of Cases
29%	47%	13%	11%	(764)

Burden of Taxation

Some people feel that they pay more taxes than they should considering what they get from government. How do you feel about this?

Taxes too high	Taxes about right	Taxes low	Don't know; Not ascertained	Number of Cases
41%	45%	2%	12%	(764)

Government Red Tape

As we know, all government bureaus have some red tape. On the whole, how much do you feel is really necessary?

Less than ½ or none	About ½	More than ½ or most	Don't know; Not ascertained	Number of Cases
47%	5%	33%	15%	(764)

status minority group pressing for more governmental action (not enough government welfare services: Negroes 61 per cent as compared with 37 per cent for the white population). Young people also tended to demand an extension of the scope of government; age differences, however, were conditioned to some extent by the high concentration of "don't knows" among the older people (see Table VIII).

The Worth of Government

Investigation of the third dimension of self-interest, the worth of government, revealed in contrast to the other two dimensions the relative absence of a perspective appropriate for administrative behavior based on consent. Our investigation of self-interest seemed to produce relatively reasoned and reflective judgments. In the United States, however, the

TABLE VIII

GROUP DIFFERENCES IN PERSPECTIVES ON THE SCOPE
OF GOVERNMENT WELFARE SERVICES
(In per cent)

Social Characteristics	Scope of Government Welfare Services					
	Too much activity	About right; pro-con	Not enough activity	Don't know; not ascertained	Total	Number of Cases*
Social Class						
Lower Lower .	3	42	49	6	100	(250)
Upper Lower..	5	45	44	6	100	(207)
Lower Middle	9	51	31	9	100	(186)
Upper Middle	16	50	26	8	100	(106)
Negro–White						
White	8	48	37	7	100	(658)
Negro	1	33	61	5	100	(106)
Age						
21–29	3	48	45	4	100	(174)
30–39	6	45	45	4	100	(214)
40–49	8	44	45	3	100	(142)
50–59	10	46	33	11	100	(113)
60 and over ...	9	48	25	18	100	(121)

*Totals under social class include 15 cases for which social class could not be ascertained.

governmental process operates in the context of "free enterprise" and a system of business values. In the absence of the feudal tradition of Western Europe, there is little reverence for the public bureaucracy either per se or on the basis of its pragmatic authority. In the system of business values, all things have a price or a calculus of monetary worth. Somehow, the public feels, this calculus ought to apply to the government services. Since this calculus does not directly apply, or, since the average citizen is not equipped to make such judgments, self-interest perspectives, when probed in terms of economic worth or organizational efficiency, revealed more pronounced levels of hostility toward the symbols of administrative authority. By probing public perspectives on the basis of the worth of government services, taxation, and the "red tape" involved in administration, increasing kinds of hostility could be mobilized (Table VII).[5]

The persons interviewed, therefore, were asked to weigh the worth of the help and services that government provides in the light of the burdens and sacrifices that government "makes people carry."[6] Negativism and anti-governmental sentiment increased markedly. Instead of the 7 per cent of the population who felt that the scope of governmental welfare activities was too much, 29 per cent of the sample now felt that the government asks more from the public than it gives in help and services. When the question of taxes was introduced into the calculation, negativism was even more pronounced. Forty-one per cent thought taxes were too high, "considering what they get from the government." Finally, the calculus of costs permitted the strongest expression of hostility toward the bureaucracy on the subject of efficiency. Forty-seven per cent thought that less than half or none of the "red tape" in government bureaus was really necessary. (As will be discussed in Chapter IV, these feelings about "red tape" were separable

[5]These questions were not asked in battery form but were inserted in the appropriate sections of the interview schedule.

[6]The text of the question used in probing attitudes concerning the worth of government is reported in Table VII.

from favorable feelings toward the civil servant as a person.)

These higher levels of hostility do not negate the essential acceptance of the public bureaucracy. Rather, they represent ambivalence toward public authority. Negativism toward governmental authority has been an historical theme in the American pattern of values. The growth of services provided by government has undoubtedly been accompanied by increased acceptance of the symbols of government. Yet one would expect that increased acceptance of governmental authority would carry with it powerful ambivalences and residues of earlier negativism. And it would indeed be strange if these residues were not couched in the language of business ethics— cost and efficiency. These ambivalances and residues supply the raw material for election campaigns and help explain why anti-bureaucratic themes still have such currency in political competition.

The next step in the analysis of self-interest perspectives was to ascertain whether feelings of thwarted self-interest were concentrated in a particular social grouping and were thereby potentially more disruptive politically.

SOCIAL STRUCTURE AND THWARTED SELF-INTEREST

Contrary to our expectation, dissatisfaction with the burdens of government was found most heavily concentrated in the lower lower class (Table IX). In the upper lower and middle classes around 20 per cent felt that government burdens outweighed government services (government asks more), whereas 41 per cent of the lower lower class were of this opinion. The percentage of dissatisfaction in the upper lower class was very similar to the percentages for the lower and upper middle classes and reflected the sharp social division in the American working class and the closeness of the top of the working class to the middle class.

The belief that the public gets more from government than it extracts ranged from 9 per cent in the lower lower class to 18 per cent in the lower and upper middle classes, again demonstrating that favorable position in the social structure conduces to an acceptance of the worth of administrative costs.

The racial division of the metropolitan community also highlights the social sources of dissatisfaction with the burdens of government and pinpoints the sources of thwarted self-interest (Table IX). The Negro population expressed the highest level of dissatisfaction of any group (52 per cent); in fact among the lower lower class, the level of dissatisfaction among Negroes rose to 59 per cent. (The differences in levels both of satisfaction and dissatisfaction between Negroes and whites are most marked and statistically significant.)

The differences in age groups are interesting, although no simple pattern emerges (Table IX). In contrast to older age groups, especially those over fifty, there is a tendency for younger age groups to believe that government services are worth the burdens imposed. This was anticipated, especially since the young people are more disposed to extending the scope of government and on most political studies show that they are more liberal. Most noteworthy among older people, especially among those over 60, was the high concentration of no opinions. Thus, their lack of a positive feeling about the worth of government does not seem to have resulted in greater negativism but in greater indifference. To some extent the benefits that old people over 65 actually receive may be tempering their antipublic bureaucracy perspective, or at least neutralizing it.

The striking conclusion to be reached from these data is that the lower social strata and the lesser status groups demand an extension of the scope of government welfare services and yet simultaneously feel that the burdens imposed by government are not worth the services rendered. These opinions cannot be viewed as merely inconsistent. They represent the demands and pressures on the government that the submerged groups have made and will continue to make in the name of their self-interest.

A final question needs to be asked in connection with this aspect of self-interest. What accounts for the greater negativism toward the worth of government in the lower social strata?

TABLE IX

GROUP DIFFERENCES IN PERSPECTIVES ON THE WORTH OF GOVERNMENT

(In per cent)

Social Characteristics	Worth of Government				Total	Number of Cases*
	Govt services are worth (equal to) burdens	Government asks more	Public gets more	Don't know; not ascertained		
Social Class						
Lower Lower	40	41	9	10	100	(250)
Upper Lower	54	23	13	10	100	(207)
Lower Middle	48	23	18	11	100	(186)
Upper Middle	53	19	18	10	100	(106)
Negro–White						
White	51	25	13	11	100	(658)
Negro	25	52	12	11	100	(106)
Age						
21–29	51	32	14	3	100	(174)
30–39	55	28	12	5	100	(214)
40–49	51	30	12	7	100	(142)
50–59	35	33	14	18	100	(113)
60 and over	34	20	16	30	100	(121)

*Totals under social class include 15 cases for which social class could not be ascertained.

Was it not to be expected that these social groupings would more favorably evaluate the worth of government services? Was it not the case that important aspects of the public bureaucracy which operate in the metropolitan community have developed rapidly in the last three decades in response to the unsolved social conflicts and insecurities which the lower social groupings must face?

Our data reveal some tentative findings which are mainly negative. Could the actual contact and impact of these new integrative functions of government lie at the root of social class basis of self-interest patterns? Although some differences among social classes were found, we have seen that the patterns of public contacts of mass welfare agencies cut rather evenly across class lines. Thus, mere patterns of contact with administrative agencies per se would not account for the social class pattern of feelings of self-interest.

Moreover, when an index of contact with the nine other administrative agencies was broken down by social class, the differences tended to be minimized rather than accentuated (Table X). Contact with these agencies has come to have

TABLE X

SOCIAL CLASS BY EXTENT OF CONTACT WITH NINE SELECTED
PUBLIC AGENCIES IN THE DETROIT METROPOLITAN AREA
(In per cent)

Number of Agencies Contacted	Social Class				
	Lower Lower	Upper Lower	Lower Middle	Upper Middle	Total*
None or one.........	10	11	8	10	10
Two	18	18	13	18	17
Three	22	21	17	17	20
Four	23	18	25	20	22
Five...............	13	13	18	12	14
Six or more	11	16	13	18	13
Not ascertained	3	3	6	5	4
	100	100	100	100	100
Number of cases	(250)	(207)	(186)	(106)	(764)

*Includes 15 cases for which social class could not be ascertained.

more of a mass than a class character. While contact with a specific agency might condition attitudes toward that agency, gross patterns of agency contact are so general as not to be crucial variables in conditioning public perspectives.

These observations do alter the fact that for specific agencies the class basis of contact and access varies and that agency benefits are differentially distributed. Even perspectives toward the functions of specific agencies vary by social class. For example, the lower class tends to differ from the middle class in its estimate of the most important functions of the police. Or, the differential class usage of the public libraries and the public educational system can be clearly recognized. Undoubtedly, extremely depressed and slum areas are underserved by the metropolitan bureaucracy. Nevertheless, most of the social structure, and not merely these lower social strata, have developed a positive stake in the present welfare functions of the expanded public bureaucracy. The lower social strata, however, demand more government services and are more dissatisfied with the present allocation of burdens.

One might argue that the public bureaucracy should discriminate in favor of these lowest social class groupings in order to eliminate the tendency of these groups to believe that the public bureaucracy is not supporting their special needs. Only if all class groups revealed similar estimates of the worth of government services could we say that theoretically public perspectives were completely conducive to democratic consent. This would seem to be a utopian goal. The present class differences in hostility toward the worth of government services, however, do not appear to be so disruptive that they cannot be handled within the framework of contemporary political and administrative practices.

In summary, if individual self-interest implies acceptance of the current performance of governmental agencies or agreement about the scope of welfare functions, the second criterion for administrative behavior based on consent is satisfied to a considerable degree. This is in contradistinction to the first criterion where an inadequate level of knowledge was encountered.

IV

PRINCIPLE MINDEDNESS: MORALITY IN ADMINISTRATION

PUBLIC PERSPECTIVES toward administrative authority are not conditioned solely by the functions government performs. The image of governmental administration rests also on beliefs about the fairness and the "morality" with which public officials perform their duties.

Does the public believe that public servants are guided in their actions by rules which guarantee impartiality and minimize favoritism? Does the public believe that governmental agencies are run by persons who are principle-minded and not capricious or arbitrary? By principle mindedness, we mean that the administrative system operates promptly in response to individual needs without corruption, with equal and fair treatment, and without undue consideration of a person's professional agents or of his political affiliation.

Acceptance of the operations of public bureaucracy hardly guarantees that the public views the administrative system as operating on the basis of principles. A person could express a basic satisfaction with the administrative authority even though he was aware and tolerant of administrative corruption and arbitrary political favoritism. He might be forced into such a view by the belief that public administration, because it is public, can operate only with corruption and political favoritism. Another perspective, which accepts both the administrative system and favoritism, might rest simply on the belief that human nature prevents equal treatment before the law.

The criterion of principle mindedness is an additional component of a model of administration based on democratic consent. No system of administration based on consent can proceed merely on the reasonableness of men. Some set of principles, therefore, must operate to insure consistency in administrative behavior and the public must believe that such principles effectively influence the public bureaucracy.

45

Thus, we can state the third requirement for administration in a democratic political system:

For administrative behavior to be based on democratic consent, the public must be of the general opinion that the bureaucracy is guided in its actions by a set of principles. Administrative routines, however, must take into consideration individual differences to insure adequate dealings with clients.

To investigate public perspectives related to this criterion, we focused our interest on perspectives toward civil servants and administrative agencies in general; we did not consider specific government agencies.

Moreover, it seemed reasonable to assume that a person's beliefs about principle mindedness in public administration would reflect his underlying attitudes and philosophy toward government and politics. A person who believed, in general, that public officials had principles would also tend to believe that the public bureaucracy could be controlled by the political parties and by the efforts of citizen group representation. Such a person would have strong rather than weak political convictions. He would be an individual with some measure of self-confidence in political matters.

This line of reasoning implies that social psychological mechanisms would be at work in conditioning perspectives of principle mindedness. Social psychological theory maintains that, in general, a person who lacks self-confidence projects his weakness and scapegoats authority. Weak political motives and weak political self-confidence lead a person to attribute undesirable characteristics to administrative authority and to public officials. We sought, therefore, to investigate the hypothesis that weak political self-confidence goes hand in hand with the scapegoating of public officials as corrupt, dishonest, or at least accessible by means of political pull.[1]

Since we were concerned with probing for stereotypes, the

---

[1] A postwar study of perspectives in Darmstadt is the only known effort to investigate the working of social psychological predispositions in conditioning images of governmental administration. Klaus A. Lindemann, *Behörde und Bürger: Das Verhältnis zwischen Verwaltung und Bevölkerung in einer deutschen Mittelstadt* (Darmstadt, Germany: Edward Roether Verlag, 1952).

methodology of the sample survey was rather well adapted for
investigating the extent and dimensions of principle mindedness.
The images that emerged point to an unanticipated pattern.
Belief in the existence of widespread administrative corruption
and dishonesty was indeed the attitude only of a minority.
On the other hand, the view that political favoritism—political
pull—played a part in access to administrative agencies was
much more pervasive; indeed it was a majority image. The
dynamics of this apparent contradiction throws light on the
public's view of morality in government.

CORRUPTION VERSUS POLITICAL PULL

Attitudes concerning administrative corruption were investigated both generally and specifically. To probe generalized
attitudes of corruption, the following question was asked:

How many of the higher government officials would you say are
probably dishonest and corrupt—many of them, just a few, or none
at all?

Only 13 per cent said many of them, 71 per cent just a few
of them, and 7 per cent none of them (Table XI).[2] The authors
had anticipated that a higher percentage of the population
would have answered "many of them." Simply on the basis
of the existing pressures for irrational judgments that exist in
modern society, it would be difficult to expect a much lower
percentage.

A specific question on corruption in the collection of taxes
was included since, at the time of the survey, allegations about
the Bureau of Internal Revenue were still featured in the mass
media of communication. When queried concerning corruption in the collection of taxes, only 4 per cent thought "a great
deal," while another 15 per cent said "some or a little." This
total percentage is close to that encountered on the question
of corruption among high government officials. Another 10

[2]It should be noted that the question presented fixed alternatives and the first
one was "many of them." The approach was to maximize the opportunity for
expression of negative attitudes.

TABLE XI

ATTITUDES CONCERNING MORALITY IN ADMINISTRATION

Dishonesty and Corruption

How many of the higher government officials would you say are probably dishonest and corrupt—many of them, just a few, or none at all?

	Number	Per Cent
Many of them	96	13
Just a few of them	543	71
None of them	50	7
No opinion; not ascertained	75	9
Total........................	764	100

Political Pull

Some people think political pull plays an important part in whether the government will help a private citizen with some problems he has; other people don't think so. In your opinion, does political pull play an important part in whether the government will help a private citizen?

	Number	Per Cent
Yes, it plays an important part.........	311	41
Yes, it plays some part	215	28
Depends	27	4
No	113	15
No opinion; not ascertained	98	13
Total........................	764	100

per cent said there was corruption but did not specify the extent. In retrospect, it should be pointed out that this question, though carefully pretested, probably did not adequately serve its objective. For example, since the question explicitly mentioned the collection of taxes, respondents should only have considered the role of officials; it appears, however, that the answers included estimates of corruption on the part of the taxpayers.

By contrast, the overwhelming majority of the sample felt that political pull substantially affects government decisions to help private citizens with individual problems. Fifteen per cent answered no to this question; 41 per cent said yes, it plays an important part; and 28 per cent said yes, it plays some part (Table XI). Consequently, almost 70 per cent felt that political pull played an important part in helping a private citizen secure aid from the administrative system—hardly indicative of a pervasive feeling that public officials are motivated by principle mindedness.

The spontaneous remarks of those interviewed supplied revealing clues as to the meaning attributed to "political pull." Although the interview schedule did not intensively probe attitudes toward political pull, it was clear that there was little spontaneous disapproval of this form of political favoritism. Instead, it was taken for granted. Even those who denied the importance of political pull expressed their opinions with some hesitation. For example, an elementary school teacher, now married to a successful financial analyst employed by one of the automobile manufacturers in Detroit, explained:

. . . A few isolated cases but as a general rule I'd say no. Maybe I'm being very naive, but I haven't had too much to do with it . . . .

Political favoritism, among those who acknowledged its importance, was not linked to the advantages of party affiliation. It seemed rather to mean personal connections; that is, favoritism based on who knows whom. The comments of a 26-year-old recently married housewife, whose husband was a successful insurance salesman, were typical of the acceptance of personal connections. When asked about the importance of political pull in getting help from a government agency, she replied:

Well, I don't know whether I'd call it political pull—but if he has some help, if there is someone he knows, he'd get it done a lot sooner.

In short, "political pull" seemed to her too strong a term for what had become accepted practice.

Those few who candidly spoke as if they had an inside view of political pull described it mainly as a means of expediting administrative action rather than as a form of dishonesty or corruption. A 65-year-old real estate broker, who was a long-time resident of Detroit and whose income was high enough that he refused to report it to the interviewer, said:

Sometimes strings must be pulled, other times it is not necessary. . . . In the final analysis I believe pull plays very little part as far as actual help obtained. Political pull might play the big part in getting to the right place or to the right person in order to get the problem before the right person without too much delay.

No doubt such perspectives involve some rationalizations, as reflected by the inside view of an efficient and "worldly" 30-year-old female private secretary who, with matter of factness, reported:

Now, do you want that honestly or idealistically? I work for a firm that uses political pull to get contracts. It might hurry matters, but it is no more help than getting things done sooner.

Some of the condemnation of political pull was that of the detached wise guy, the over-cynical variety: "Everything is politics: it's all political pull." The real inner feelings of these persons in effect were undiscovered. Some of the outright condemnation of political pull, however, was of an extreme nature, often reflecting personal emotional involvements and highly individualized circumstances difficult to assess. For example, a 45-year-old woman of lower middle class background, whose husband is an underpaid sales manager, blurted out:

Yes, my mother was killed in an auto accident and we weren't able to prosecute the man because he had political affiliations. It was a very bitter experience. It's too true! As far as I know he's never been put where he should be.

Thus, aside from the minority who condemned it, political pull and political favoritism were, so to speak, the advantages other persons were alleged to have in dealing with the administrative behemoth. It was viewed as a human and understandable way of coping with and adapting to complexity and impersonality. The image of political pull involved a popular conception of the bureaucracy's response to organized pressure and group representation.

Perhaps it is a contemporary form of political realism to evaluate the administrative performance of the individual civil servant favorably and, at the same time, accept political pull as significant. Widespread belief in the importance of political favoritism appears to be compatible with a high level of satisfaction about personal dealings with public employees. In our

sample, 17 per cent thought that their personal dealings with public employees were very good, 48 per cent good, 22 per cent fair, and 6 per cent poor.[3]

To state the matter alternatively, individual beliefs about the importance of political pull were reflected in markedly differing estimates of the quality of individual dealings with public employees.[4]

In this connection, there is some evidence that the civil servants and employees of a large private firm may be similarly evaluated. The question was asked of our sample: "Would you say that generally you get more courteous attention in dealing with city employees than in dealing with employees of big companies?" The responses encountered were: city employees more courteous, 27 per cent; both equally courteous, 29 per cent; private employees more courteous, 24 per cent. At different points in the interview materials, the feeling emerged that impersonality and red tape were not exclusive problems of government agencies.

Thus, the quality of personal dealings with public employees was not a major source of hostility toward the public bureaucracy. Nor, strangely enough, was it an explanation of why persons felt that political pull was an important factor in getting assistance from the public bureaucracy. In part, each person may merely have distinguished the performance of the individual civil servant from that of administrative agencies.

[3]Satisfaction with personal dealings with public employees is relatively high and there is some evidence that this represents a long-term trend. On the basis of a comparison of the Detroit Area Study data with Professor L. D. White's research, responses to the question, "In general, would you say that your dealings with public employees were poor, fair, good, or very good?" showed a noticeable improvement. The unfavorable category (poor) dropped from 24 per cent in the Chicago study to 6 per cent in the Detroit Area Study. To the 6 per cent of the public who said their dealings were poor, another 22 per cent said fair, while the majority of the population designated their relations as good or very good. The problem of comparison of our data with Professor White's findings is discussed in Chapter V.

[4]Certain attitudes toward the public service were conditioned by the fact that an individual was employed by the public service or was in a family who had a member in the public service. Belief in the importance of political pull was not influenced by this variable.

The average civil servant with whom the public deals could be evaluated as decent and adequate. But the large and impersonal organization could be blamed for the necessity of political pull.

Direct evidence emerged from our interview which underlines the overwhelming extent to which the public feels itself unable and unequipped to approach directly the agencies of government. Only 16 per cent of the sample would approach a government agency directly with an individual problem (see Table XII). Those in this group often manifested a general rebelliousness rather than personal self-assuredness. Thus, a 43-year-old spinster, born in Macon and now employed in the postal system, tersely replied, "I fight my own battles."

On the other hand, 75 per cent expressed a recognition of the need for intermediaries, professional or organizational. "I think it's better to have an organization behind you. My husband goes through the VFW," claimed a 23-year-old housewife, a native of Detroit, whose husband was in training for the police force. As was expected, lawyers and accountants were most frequently mentioned as potential intermediaries: 26 per cent (see Table XII). Organizations were the next most frequent: 16 per cent. Even in the Detroit area, interestingly enough, trade unions did not figure prominently. Government officials, elected and administrative, received somewhat fewer mentions: 13 per cent. The political party has lost many of its functions as an intermediary between the public and administrative agencies; professional and special interest groups have assumed this function. In short, the view of the necessity of political pull in gaining access to governmental agencies seems closely linked to the general difficulties the individual citizen feels he has in approaching the agencies of government.

POLITICAL PULL AND SELF-CONFIDENCE

We believe that personality and social psychological mechanisms are at the root of beliefs about morality in administration. The image of political favoritism is thought to be psychologically

TABLE XII

ATTITUDES CONCERNING ACCESS TO GOVERNMENT AGENCIES

In general, if you had a problem to take up with a government bureau, would you do it yourself or do you think you would be better off if you got the help of some person or organization?

	Number	Per Cent
Would do it himself	123	16
Would try to do it himself; then get outside help..................	60	8
Would get help of an outsider	453	59
Depends	87	11
Not ascertained	41	5
Total	764	100

Type of Intermediary in Dealing with Government Agencies:

Professional	Number	Per Cent
Lawyer, Accountant	199	26
Minister, Pastor, Priest	14	2
	213	28
Organizational		
Voluntary	106	14
Trade Unions	12	2
	118	16
Governmental		
Elected Officials	63	8
Governmental Official	38	5
	101	13
Personal		
Friends or Relatives	52	7
Not applicable; do it himself................	123	16
Don't know; not ascertained	157	20
	764	100
Total...................................		

linked to the tensions and problems which the individual experiences in dealing with an administrative organization which is extensive and impersonal. It seemed, therefore, that the social psychological concept of political self-confidence might help to explain these perspectives with their stereotypic overtones. Political self-confidence is a measure of the individual's estimate of his (the self's) ability to influence political events. Research has shown that political self-confidence is positively associated with high and persistent voting behavior. Political self-confidence reflects a person's estimate of his own capacity to cope with political realities. Thus, the concept of political self-confidence ought to clarify views about the role of political pull. A person lacking political self-confidence in dealing with the complexity of an impersonal bureaucracy might be expected to claim the importance of political pull. More precisely, the hypothesis was investigated that strong feelings of political self-confidence would be inversely related to the belief that political pull was necessary in dealing with the public bureaucracy.

Political self-confidence was measured as low, medium, and high on the basis of a Guttman-type scale of responses to the following questions:

1. So many other people vote in elections that it doesn't matter much whether I vote or not.

2. People like me don't have any say about what the government does.

3. I don't think public officials care much about what people like me think.[5]

For the entire sample the relationship between low political self-confidence and belief in the importance of political pull was not as marked as we had anticipated (Table XIII). It was more important among those with extreme attitudes. Fifty-five per cent of those with low political self-confidence expressed the belief that political pull played an important part; among those with high political self-confidence the figure dropped to 38 per cent, a statistically significant difference. It should be pointed out that there was a social class basis for

[5]These statements were on a card which had been handed to the respondent. He was asked whether he *strongly agreed, agreed, disagreed,* or *strongly disagreed* with each one. It was assumed that agreement with the statements indicated a low degree of political self-confidence while disagreement with the statements indicated a high degree of political confidence.

In operationalizing political self-confidence by means of a scale based on projective-like questions, our measure, like the most projective tests, differentiates the extremes of high and low better than those falling in the middle range. It is the case that the middle class generally manifests a higher level of self-confidence than the lower class. Likewise, it is true that education is linked to higher self-confidence. But the data from this and other studies indicate that political self-confidence does not merely reflect educated, middle-class political attitudes.

TABLE XIII

POLITICAL SELF-CONFIDENCE AND IMPORTANCE OF POLITICAL PULL
(In per cent)

Part Played by Political Pull	Political Self-confidence		
	Low	Medium	High
Yes, important part	55	36	38
Yes, some part...................	18	35	32
Depends	2	3	6
No	10	16	10
Don't know; not ascertained	15	10	5
	100	100	100
Number of cases	(201)	(207)	(314)

belief in the importance of political pull. The lower social groupings emphasized pull to a greater extent than the middle class. Those who thought political pull played an important part ranged from 46 per cent in the lower lower class to 29 per cent in the upper middle class. On the basis of our analysis of self-interest, it was to be expected that those persons at the bottom of the social pyramid would display the greatest degree of hostility and frustration in dealing with large-scale administrative organization. Nevertheless, when the social class factor was held constant the limited relationship between political pull and political self-confidence was found in both middle and lower social class groupings.

There is clearly a pressing need for more intensive research into public perspectives about the morality of public servants and the public bureaucracy. The third criterion for administration based on consent—belief in the principle mindedness of the public bureaucracy—reveals no clearcut conclusions. Our data indicate an underlying tolerance toward the public servant and a reluctance to scapegoat the public servant as corrupt. The danger seems to lie in the widespread belief that personal favoritism is a powerful advantage in securing aid from the public bureaucracy.

V

THE NEW PRESTIGE OF PUBLIC EMPLOYMENT

IN THE QUARTER of a century that has passed since Professor Leonard D. White first described the low prestige of public employment, the scope and importance of government has expanded tremendously at all levels.[1] Nevertheless, continued low prestige of public employment has remained an assumption of American political life and in the writings of political scientists. By "prestige" we mean the social reputation, respect, deference, esteem, and recognition accorded to an individual or group.

The career public administrator and the political scientist can point to the rise of the merit system and enhanced job benefits; yet both are inclined to feel that the desired goals in prestige have yet to be achieved.[2] Furthermore, recent studies, most of which have focused on the attitudes of select groups of college students toward higher level federal employment, point to the same conclusion.

Thus, in 1947 the President's Scientific Research Board reported that among a sample of scientists in the United States the desirability of government employment was lower than that of university and industrial employment.[3] In 1948, the Personnel Policy Committee of the Commission on Organization of the Executive Branch of the Government conducted surveys of college seniors' attitudes and of past and present top-level career employees which pointed to the relative prestige un-

[1]Leonard D. White, *The Prestige Value of Public Employment* (Chicago: Univ. of Chicago Press, 1929). Also by same author *Further Contributions to the Prestige Value of Public Employment* (Chicago: Univ. of Chicago Press, 1932).

[2]A comprehensive statement of this orientation was contained in an article by Lowell H. Hattery, "The Prestige of Federal Employment," *Public Administration Review*, XV (Summer 1955), pp. 181-87.

[3]*Science and Public Policy*, Vol. III, "Administration for Research" (Wash., D. C., 1947). Research on the attitudes of scientists who work only in government was done by Clark D. Ahlberg and John C. Honey, *Attitudes of Scientists and Engineers about Their Government Employment* (Syracuse, N. Y.: Syracuse University, 1950). These authors summarized their findings in "The Scientist's Attitude Toward Government Employment," *Science*, CXIII (May 4, 1951), pp. 505-10.

attractiveness of a career in the federal government.[4] Two more recent studies which focused on college seniors also pointed to the relatively low prestige of public employment as compared with private employment.[5]

But what are the attitudes of the population at large toward government employment? Was there any reason to assume that the public at large would have different attitudes from those of selected groups of college students? Are not the public's attitudes dependent on traditional stereotypes of the government service and not on its personal experiences? Have not the mass media, especially the newspapers, continued to approach the public service with deep mistrust and negativism? Have not the various legislative committees investigating the civil service had primary objectives other than that of raising the prestige of public employment? Only by cross-sectional studies of the total population can we hope to understand the broad context and emerging trends in attitudes toward the prestige of public employment. Public perspectives at large are required to apply our fourth criterion concerning administrative behavior based on democratic consent:

> *For administrative behavior to be based on democratic consent, public perspectives toward the public bureaucracy must include adequate prestige value toward employment as compared with other types of careers. Both very low prestige and very high prestige would interfere with the bureaucracy's ability to operate on the basis of democratic consent.*

From the point of view of internal management, the prestige value of public employment is crucial. Low prestige of public employment is a barrier to effective recruitment and to the

[4]*Report of the Personnel Policy Committee*, Commission on the Organization of the Executive Branch of the Government, Appendix C, "Studies in the Prestige of Federal Employment" (Wash., D. C.: October 1948, mimeographed).

[5]George P. Bush, *Engineering Students and Federal Employment* (Wash., D. C.: American University, 1951). A summary of the findings may be found in *Science*, CXIV (Nov. 2, 1951), pp. 445-58, "Federal Recruitment of Junior Engineers," by George P. Bush and Lowell H. Hattery.

Charles M. Hersh, *College Seniors and Federal Employment* (Wash., D. C.: American University, 1953). A summary of the study appears in *Science*, Vol. 120 (July 2, 1954), pp. 12-14, "Attitudes of College Seniors toward Federal and Industrial Employment," by Charles M. Hersh and Lowell H. Hattery.

maintenance of employee morale. In the words of Professor White:

> Intangible though it is, prestige is a commodity of value in the art of management. Fundamentally management is the manipulation of external conditions and of individual and group attitudes for the purpose of securing and maintaining a social-psychological situation favorable to the accomplishment of the end sought by the organization—industrial, educational, clerical, or governmental, as the case may be. Prestige is one of the attitudes which may help or hinder the task of management.[6]

Likewise, from the external viewpoint—the direct linkages between governmental bureaucracy and the public—the prestige of the civil service is of central concern. If the public servant has very low prestige, his ability to command the consent of the public is seriously limited. Prestige is a quality assigned on the basis of a range of attributes. Prestige of the civil servant derives, no doubt, from the functions government performs, from the image of desirability of a career in government, and from the interpersonal relations of an individual with government agencies and agents. The importance of prestige here is that it is an essential element of public authority. Where administrative regulations and procedures are to be enforced with minimum coercion, low prestige of public employment is a hindrance. The public servant must fall back on his coercive power and his ultimate sanctions, with the result not only of undermining organizational efficiency, but also of straining the political fabric of society. The public service with very low prestige tends to be of the "subservient" type. It is unable to make its contribution to the resolution of conflict in the social structure and it is unable to maintain its own fundamental organizational objectives.

Theoretically, the possibility exists that too high prestige of the public service could operate as an obstruction to the democratic political system. The position of the German civil service throughout most of its history is a classic example of

---

[6]White, *Further Contributions to the Prestige Value of Public Employment*, p. 87.

this point. Excessively high prestige for the public service might produce the situation in which the government would tend to have a monopoly in the recruitment of new talent—indeed, a purely hypothetical set of circumstances for public administration in a free enterprise society. The administrator who belongs to a public service with excessive high prestige may well tend to become despotic, arbitrary, and authoritarian. The need for cultivating the consent of his clients is absent, and administration tends to proceed by military-like decree. In a democratic political system, the disruptive dangers of excessively high prestige may be limited to specific agencies in the public bureaucracy, rather than in the bureaucracy as a whole.

In the past, the low prestige of public employment has contributed to the imbalance in administrative behavior in the United States. It is important that the empirical findings of the Detroit Area Study call into question the presumed low prestige of public employment. The findings indicate, instead, a marked increase in its prestige value since the period of Professor White's investigations in Chicago. His findings, as well as those of the Detroit Area Study, refer to the esteem or the respect which the population has for public employment and the public service. They do not focus on the prestige of high level administrators or specialists in the public service. In assessing these findings, all of which point to a long-term trend in the direction of satisfying this criterion of administrative behavior in a democratic society, there is no assurance that adequate levels of prestige have been achieved for all levels of the public bureaucracy.

TREND LINES: 1929–54

There was good reason to believe that we would find a marked increase in the prestige value of public employment over the last twenty-five years. The basis for predicting an increase in the prestige of public employment was two-fold and had to do with long-term trends in American society:

1. It was assumed that, for important sections of the population in a metropolitan community, underlying attitudes toward the public service would be conditioned by the operation of new government service. The expansion of governmental services has meant that real benefits are now conferred on wide segments of the population which would, in the long run, result in an increase in positive attitudes towards those responsible. Thus, the long-term changes of the character of government through the New Deal and postwar periods would be more important than the impact of the mass media or the character of political debate about the public bureaucracy.

2. The last twenty-five years have witnessed a shift in the dominant values attached to occupational careers; job security has become a dominant value. The public's images of the job security of public employment would be likely to enhance the respect and esteem for the civil servant's career. Thus, on both these counts we expected to find, just as Professor White found, that the social groups with low income, low education, and low social status would have the highest respect for public employment. Comparatively, these groups could be assumed to have gained the most as a result of the new services of government and, in addition, these are the groups most concerned with job security.

Although our interview investigated a range of topics beyond Professor White's original objectives, special care was taken to duplicate closely some of his key questions and thereby enhance the possibility of comparison.[7] In particular, we used as a

[7]Professor White sought to investigate attitudes of the representative public and although he lacked refined sampling procedures, the controls he applied render his findings most useful for comparative purposes. White and his associates secured interviews from as many and as varied groups as was administratively possible. The sample was overweighted with young people and college students. In his analysis White attempted to compensate for this unrepresentativeness by adjusting his prestige index to approximate the true character of the Chicago population's attitude toward the prestige of public service. Any spurious results traceable to the sampling bias present in the Chicago study would reinforce statements about the rise in prestige of public employment. The large proportion of young persons and students in the Chicago sample would bias the results against the public service. The actual attitudes of Chicagoans toward public employment were probably more negative than White reported. Thus, the improve-

point of departure his insight that charting the prestige of public employment in the United States meant comparing the public's evaluation of occupations in the public service with the same ones in private employment.

In brief, our findings indicate that prestige of public employment has moved into a new phase and lost much of its "second class citizen" status. The finding of Professor White that, for the population at large, private employment per se holds higher esteem is no longer true. This conclusion derives not from an isolated finding but from numerous aspects of the Detroit Area Study, from comparisons with Professor White's findings, and from two national opinion surveys. Currently, in the Detroit metropolitan area, opinion on the general question: "If the pay were the same, would you prefer to work for the United States government or for a private firm," reveals a preference for governmental employment (Table XIV). Fifty-six per cent of the total population selected government and 30 per cent industry, while the remaining 14 per cent were indifferent or had no opinion.

TABLE XIV

TREND IN PREFERENCE FOR GOVERNMENT VERSUS PRIVATE EMPLOYMENT*
(In per cent)

Preference	US National Survey (Fortune) February 1940	US National Survey (AIPO) August 1947	Detroit Area Study February 1954
U. S. government	40	41	56
Private firm	50	40	30
No preference; no opinion	10	19	14
	100	100	100

*February Survey, 1940, *Fortune* Poll: Would you prefer the government or private business as an employer?" August Survey, 1947, American Institute of Public Opinion: "Assuming the pay is the same, would you prefer to work for the U. S. government or for a private firm?"

ment in prestige during the years intervening between the Chicago and Detroit studies is probably greater than the comparative results suggest. All comparisons are made in the light of differences in sampling and minor modifications in wording of questions.

The responses of an urban area as compared to a rural area were expected to be more favorable to government employment; perhaps also the unstable conditions of the Detroit labor market increased the percentage who selected government employment over other areas in the country. Nevertheless, the Detroit Area Study data confirm the findings of other national surveys which not only indicate improved prestige of government employment but underline the fact that this development has been in process for a number of years (Table XIV). In 1940, the *Fortune* Survey found in a national survey that 50 per cent selected private employment, while by 1947 the American Institute of Public Opinion recorded only 40 per cent as more favorable to private employment.

Next, it was possible to compare these trends with the state of public opinion in two other democracies, Canada and Australia, where under British influence the development of the civil service is presumed to have gone further. Contrary to our expectation, the prestige of public employment was not markedly higher in either Australia or Canada (Table XV). In all these four surveys, the question assumed pay to be equal and therefore responses focused directly on the prestige value

TABLE XV

PREFERENCE FOR GOVERNMENT VERSUS PRIVATE EMPLOYMENT:
NATIONAL COMPARISONS*

(In per cent)

Preference	Australia 1948	Canada 1948	United States 1947	Detroit Area 1954
Government	44	36	41	56
Private	47	45	40	30
No difference	5	2†	...	...
No opinion; undecided	4	17	19	14
	100	100	100	100

*Australia Public Opinion Polls, July 1948: "If two jobs had the same wages and conditions, but one was with the government and the other in a private business, which would you choose?" Canadian Institute for Public Opinion, March 1948: "Assuming that the pay is the same, would you prefer to work for the Dominion government or a private firm?"

†Answer: "If the other party were in power."

of public employment. Contrary to current assumptions concerning federal employment prestige among public administration experts, it can be said that in the United States, where business values are presumed to dominate, the prestige of public employment is at least as high as in Canada and Australia.

Now we can turn to the direct comparison between Professor White's findings and our data on the basis of the preferences for specific occupations in private industry versus government employment. Again, the results confirm at all points the trend toward higher prestige of public employment. The specific group of occupations in the public service under investigation in the Detroit Area Study had on the basis of Professor White's method of computation an over-all prestige index of −2.5 which was markedly higher than the −11.7 index for a similar group of occupations in 1929 in Chicago.[8] In neither Professor White's research nor in our survey was there any special interest in the specific jobs of the general administrator type. Instead the focus was on the broad range of skills which make up the bulk of public service. White investigated a battery of occupational roles from janitor to chemist. The relative prestige of public employment varied from job to job, yet the lower prestige of government regardless of the job was generally present. The sampling of a comparable but much smaller list of specific occupations hardly presented the same pattern in the Detroit Area Study (Table XVI).[9] Interestingly enough, it was only in the case of the doctor, with his specific role in our society, that private employment was more esteemed than government service (53 per cent to 25 per cent). In one case, that of stenographer, a sizable plurality (49 per cent to 25 per cent) accorded public employment more esteem than private employment. In two cases (accountant and night watchman)

[8]White, *The Prestige Value of Public Employment.* The prestige index is the difference between the percentage of total choices favoring public employment and the percentage of total choices favoring private employment.

[9]Doctor, accountant, stenographer, and night watchman were used in order to cover job classifications which have high, middle range, and low intrinsic prestige.

TABLE XVI

Prestige of Selected Occupations in Government and
Private Employment*

(In per cent)

Type of Employment	Occupation			
	Stenographer	Accountant	Watchman	Doctor
Public	49	38	35	25
No difference or don't know	22	18	20	17
Private	25	39	40	53
Not ascertained	4	5	5	5
	100	100	100	100
Number of Cases......	(764)	(764)	(764)	(764)

*Question asked: We'd like to know what people think of government jobs and government workers. If these jobs are about the same in kind of work, pay, and so forth, which have the most prestige: (a) a stenographer in a life insurance company or a stenographer in the city tax assessor's office; (b) an accountant in the Detroit Department of Public Works or an accountant in a private accounting firm; (c) a night watchman in a bank or a night watchman in City Hall; (d) a doctor in the Detroit Receiving Hospital or a doctor who is on the staff of a private hospital.

the attractiveness of private industry and governmental service was relatively balanced.

Additional dimensions of the enhanced reputation of the public servant emerge from the replication of two additional questions investigated by Professor White:

Would you say that generally you get more courteous attention in dealing with city employees than in dealing with employees of big companies? (See Table XVII.)

Thus, even if the "don't know" responses which were not separated in the Chicago study are considered unfavorable to the public servant—which is hardly necessary—the marked improvement is still evidenced. It seems hardly likely that this shift is entirely due to improved client relations on the part of the public service, although this factor is certainly at work. The new services that government performs also seemed involved in this attitude change. Likewise, responses to the question: "In general, would you say that your dealings with public employees were poor, fair, good, or very good," showed

TABLE XVII

ATTITUDES CONCERNING COURTESY OF PUBLIC AND PRIVATE EMPLOYEES
(In per cent)

Type of Treatment	White's Study	Detroit Area Study
Private employees, more courteous	60	29
Both equal	22	29
City employees, more courteous	18	27
Don't know; not ascertained	...	15
	100	100

a similar improvement. The unfavorable category (poor) dropped from 24 per cent in the Chicago study to 6 per cent in the Detroit study.

THE CORRELATES OF PRESTIGE

The next step in the analysis was to determine how the prestige value of public employment varied among different social groups. As stated above, we believed that we would find a higher level of esteem for public employment than a quarter of a century ago; nevertheless, we expected to find that prestige of public employment would still be highest among those very same groups that Professor White had encountered. With some minor but interesting variations, the Detroit Area Study found, as did White, that those for whom public employment had the highest prestige value tended to come from the bottom of the social structure (Table XVIII). By means of an attitude-scaling technique, it was possible to classify the sample of the Detroit metropolitan area into groups with high, middle range, and low prestige evaluation of public employment.[10]

1. Lower class position and correspondingly low income were both linked to high prestige evaluations of public employment. Moving up in the social class structure, the positive attitudes towards government employment declined and the negative ones

[10]The Guttman scaling technique was employed. The coefficient of reproducibility for the scale was .916.

TABLE XVIII

GROUP DIFFERENCES IN THE PRESTIGE VALUE OF PUBLIC EMPLOYMENT
(In per cent)

Social Characteristics	Prestige Scale					
	High	Middle	Low	Not Ascertained	Total	Number
Income						
Under 2,000	30	42	21	7	100	(81)
2,000–3,999	31	38	24	7	100	(145)
4,000–5,999	33	36	27	4	100	(269)
6,000–7,999	20	36	35	9	100	(134)
Over 8,000	15	33	44	7	100	(97)
Social Class						
Lower Lower.......	37	38	21	4	100	(250)
Upper Lower.......	31	39	26	4	100	(207)
Lower Middle......	25	32	36	7	100	(186)
Upper Middle......	14	34	43	9	100	(106)
Negro–White						
White	26	37	31	6	100	(658)
Negro	44	33	18	5	100	(106)
Sex						
Male	26	34	34	6	100	(360)
Female	31	39	24	6	100	(404)
Education						
Less than elementary	27	47	15	11	100	(105)
Elementary	25	38	24	3	100	(133)
Some high school ...	31	40	26	1	100	(173)
Completed high school	31	31	33	5	100	(236)
Some or completed college	14	34	47	5	100	(109)
*Foreign Background**						
Born in U.S. of U.S.-born father†	24	35	37	4	100	(283)
Born in U.S. of for-eign-born father† .	30	37	29	4	100	(219)
Foreign born	24	43	22	11	100	(141)

*Whites only.
†Father of the head of the household.

increased. On an income basis, the division of attitudes from more favorable toward more unfavorable occurred around the $6,000 level.

2. The difference between Negro and white attitudes was as great as any between other social groupings and revealed the attractiveness of government jobs to a low status group in particular. Clearly, the relative absence of discrimination in government employment was partly responsible. In addition to the non-discrimination policies of the federal government, the three other units of government—the state of Michigan, Wayne County, and the City of Detroit—all have well-established merit systems. Likewise, it is worthy of note that women accord higher prestige to government employment than do men. Again, no doubt at the root was a similar belief in the greater equality of treatment that the impersonal and official character of government affords.

3. At variance with the findings of the earlier study, foreign-born status was not positively linked to higher opinions of the prestige value of government employment. This finding in no way contradicts the central conclusion linking low position in the social structure and positive attitudes toward government service. It merely reaffirms that with the process of assimilation of the foreign-born, new groups such as Negroes and rural migrants now contribute heavily to the lower class of the urban industrial community.

4. Education is known to be associated with social class as well as income and, therefore, it was to be expected that the well educated held more unfavorable attitudes than those with a lower level of education. Favorable attitudes were concentrated in those with less education, but the link was not direct. Given increased education up to the completion of high school, there emerged a uniformly high concentration of individuals favorable to public employment, with the exception of those with less than eight years of schooling. Strikingly enough, only for those individuals with some college or completed college education did education reach the level where the reputation of government employment dropped off sharply. These findings raise a strong presumption about the inability of higher education to foster a more balanced evaluation of the prestige of government employment.

In addition, the influence of education emerges when the educational patterns of the lower class individual are separated from those of the middle class individual (Table XIX). Such a comparison is, in part, unequal since the lower class has limited access to higher education. But it is clear that whereas for the middle class extended education, especially at the college level, was sharply linked to unfavorable attitudes toward government jobs, educational experience for the working class does not have this consequence.

While many specific factors may account for these group differences, they all underline the real as well as the symbolic attractiveness of a government career and job for those who find themselves at the bottom of the economic and social pyramid. Two social processes were assumed to lie at the heart of the matter. First, a government job was attractive for these groups because of the job security features that the public attributes to government employment. The reasons given by the sample in the Detroit Area Study for preferring public employment in general over private employment were predominately based on this feature (73 per cent gave job security or job retirement benefits as their reasons for preferring government

TABLE XIX

PRESTIGE OF PUBLIC EMPLOYMENT, SOCIAL CLASS, AND EDUCATION LEVEL
(In per cent)

Level of Education	Prestige Scale					
	High	Middle	Low	Not Ascertained	Total	Number
Lower Class						
Some elementary ...	33	44	16	7	100	(107)
Completed elementary	33	41	25	1	100	(83)
Some high school ...	36	37	23	4	100	(131)
High school or more.	34	34	29	3	100	(131)
Middle Class						
Some high school ...	23	40	29	8	100	(78)
High school	26	29	38	7	100	(130)
Attended college ...	11	32	51	6	100	(81)

employment). The next most frequent response (6 per cent) was that public personnel policies were fairer. On the other hand, red tape and bureaucratic procedures of government employment were given as the main reason by those who preferred private employment (26 per cent). A reason given almost as frequently was "more opportunity for advancement" (21 per cent). These are entrepeneurial goals which one would expect to condition a preference for private employment.

The second basis for explaining the increased attractiveness of public employment was the assumption that the benefits distributed by new government services would have an effect on the prestige of public employment. Despite the complexity of this problem, direct evidence was collected indicating that underlying attitudes towards the role of government (as opposed to mere political partisanship) were involved. By means of the following question, the public's conception of the proper sphere of government was investigated:

Some people think that the national government should do more in trying to deal with such problems of unemployment, education, housing, and so on. Others think that government is already doing too much. On the whole, would you say that what the government has done has been about right, too much, or not enough?

Table XX reveals a marked and pronounced association between attitudes on the proper sphere of government action and the individual's evaluation of the prestige value of public employment. Whereas 35 per cent of those who believed that

TABLE XX

ATTITUDES TOWARD THE PROPER SCOPE OF GOVERNMENT AND THE PRESTIGE OF PUBLIC EMPLOYMENT

(In per cent)

Scope of Government	Prestige Scale					
	High	Middle	Low	Not Ascertained	Total	Number
Too much	10	33	56	2	100	(52)
About right	29	37	32	3	100	(353)
Not enough	35	38	25	2	100	(305)

government was not doing enough had high opinions of government employment, only 10 per cent of those who thought government was doing too much had similar favorable attitudes. Those who thought government was taking about the right amount of action had rather average attitudes toward public employment, while groups who believed that the government was doing too much had an overwhelmingly negative attitude. All of these data can be taken as an indication that the services of government as they actually impinge on the public condition the prestige accorded to government employment.

Finally, it seemed important to investigate the consequences of personal and family affiliation with the public bureaucracy. Did persons who worked for the government accord higher prestige to the public service than the population at large? What about persons who had immediate family members in public employment? Interestingly enough, our expectations were reversed: public employment leads persons to accord lower prestige value to public employment than other types of employment.

In all, 103 persons, or 14 per cent of the sample, could be classified as having *direct* affiliation with public employment. This group consisted of 25 persons who themselves were employed by government agencies and 78 persons who were members of households in which the head of the household or some other member was a public employee. From Table XXI it can be seen that those having direct affiliation with public employment—public employees themselves and their immedi-

TABLE XXI

AFFILIATION WITH PUBLIC EMPLOYMENT AND
THE PRESTIGE OF PUBLIC EMPLOYMENT
(In per cent)

Affiliation	Prestige Scale					
	High	Middle	Low	Not Ascertained	Total	Number
Direct affiliation	31	29	38	2	100	(103)
No direct affiliation .	28	38	28	6	100	(656)

ate kin—held public employment in lower esteem than the rest of the population (38 per cent in the low prestige category for those with direct affiliation is significantly larger than the 28 per cent found in the rest of the population).

This observation is the more striking when we take into account two considerations which are conducive to an opposite result. First, persons in general tend to overevaluate the prestige of their own occupational choice and not to underevaluate it. Second, since public employees have low incomes they would be expected to rate the prestige of private employment relatively higher, as do other groups with limited incomes. But this was not the case on both counts.

What seem to be the sources of this self-depreciation? In part the attitude seems similar to a minority group feeling of self-depreciation. The government employee feels that he is in a minority and accepts the belief that the minority status is low. He has not been able to upgrade his self-esteem and he holds on to attitudes which were appropriate a quarter of a century ago. There can be no doubt that the lack of esprit de corps and solidarity within the ranks of the civil servant is also at work. In the absence of esprit de corps and organizational solidarity, self-evaluation tends to become depressed; and in turn, low self-evaluations tend to prevent the development of higher esprit de corps and solidarity.[11]

In a very real sense, it is hoped that these findings about the rise in the prestige level of public employment may contribute to an increase of both the public servant's self-esteem and his sense of organizational solidarity.[12]

These historical trends are relevant for evaluating the fourth

[11]See William Delany, "Bureaucrat and Citizen: A Study of Government Bureaucracies in a Metropolitan Setting," (unpublished Ph.D. dissertation, Univ. of Michigan, 1957) for an analysis of these problems among three government agencies in the Detroit metropolitan area.

[12]Two recent studies underline the persistence of relative low status of the military career in American social structure. See *Attitudes of Adult Civilians Toward the Military Services as a Career* and *Attitudes of 16–20-year Old Males Toward the Military Service as a Career*, both by Public Opinion Surveys, Inc., Princeton, N. J., 1955. These studies did not focus on the status of the *higher ranking officer* groups.

criterion of administrative behavior based on consent. Both very low and very high prestige of public employment, it is asserted, would operate to interfere with the bureaucracy's ability to function on the basis of democratic consent. There is no reason to expect any sudden reversal of the present pattern of opinions in the near future. The problem appears to be that the trend toward higher prestige of government employment may well have reached a plateau and that this plateau is still below the desired level for administrative behavior based on consent.

VI

POLITICAL PARTY IDENTIFICATION AND ADMINISTRATIVE PERSPECTIVES

IN DEVELOPING our criteria of administrative behavior based on consent, we assumed that a person's perspective toward the administrative process would not coincide with his perspective toward the election arena. If attitudes toward administrative authority could be directly inferred from political partisanship, the importance and relevance of this research would have been greatly reduced.

Empirical validation of this assumption proceeded by means of the hypothesis that persons of different political identifications—Republicans and Democrats—would overlap considerably in crucial dimensions of their perspectives toward administrative authority. Because of the well-recognized diversity of opinion within political parties, there was little doubt that this would be the case. But the question was, how much overlap? Could it be the case that in a northern metropolitan community, such as Detroit, the differences *between* party adherents would be less than the range of opinion *within* each party?

THE IMPORTANCE OF PARTY PREFERENCE

To investigate this problem, the various dimensions of self-interest in administrative behavior were compared on the basis of the person's party identification. These dimensions as described in Chapter III were: (1) acceptance-rejection of administrative performance, (2) perspectives about the scope of government, and (3) evaluations of the worth of government services. Of these dimensions, the one concerning the scope of government was expected to be most closely linked with party identification since it directly implies political party preference. The results of analyzing self-interest perspective by party identification were:

1. When the scale of acceptance-rejection of administrative authority performance was broken down by social class and

party identification, the difference between Republicans and Democrats was slight indeed (Table XXII).[1]

Of the three categories—predominate acceptance, intermediate, and predominate rejection—the greatest difference was in the concentration of persons in the category of predominate acceptance: for the total sample, Republicans exceeded the Democrats by only 43 per cent to 37 per cent. This difference is hardly statistically significant. On the other hand, the differences within each party, as shown by the relative concentration of different types, were greater than the differences between parties.

When the social class basis of this attitude complex was investigated, the differences between Republican and Democratic identifiers do not increase (Table XXII). In fact, in the working class a reversal emerged, with the concentration of predominate acceptance among the Democrats just exceeding that among the Republicans (33 per cent to 31 per cent).

2. Perspectives about the scope of government revealed the greatest differences between Republicans and Democrats. Even so, the overlap between the two groups of party identifiers was, as expected, still extensive (Table XXIII).[2]

The area of agreement between Republicans and Democrats is reflected by the fact that while 58 per cent of the Republicans (somewhat more than a majority) thought that the present level of government action was about right, for the Democrats the percentage was 45 per cent (somewhat less than a majority).

[1]Party identification was determined by the question, "Generally speaking, do you consider yourself a Republican or a Democrat?" If the respondent said "Independent," he was asked, "Do you think of yourself as closer to the Republican or closer to the Democratic party?"

[2]It will be recalled that perspectives about the scope of government were investigated by the question, "Some people think the national government should do more in trying to deal with such problems as unemployment, education, housing, and so on. Others think that the government is already doing too much. On the whole, would you say that what the government has done has been about right, too much, or not enough?" The symbol "national government" was used although the functions encompassed refer to those relevant for the definition of the metropolitan community. Community based functions by state and local government would presumably produce even higher levels of agreement between Republicans and Democrats.

TABLE XXII

PERSPECTIVES TOWARD THE PERFORMANCE OF ADMINISTRATIVE AUTHORITY BY SOCIAL CLASS AND BY POLITICAL PARTY IDENTIFICATION

ACCEPTANCE–REJECTION DIMENSION

(In per cent)

Perspectives	Social Class							Scale Types*
	Working Class		Middle Class		Total Sample			
	Rep.	Dem.	Rep.	Dem.	Rep.	Ind.	Dem.	
Predominate acceptance	31	33	52	45	43	33	37	1 and 2
Intermediate	41	38	29	36	33	35	37	3 and 4
Predominate rejection	19	21	13	13	17	15	18	5 and 6
Don't know; not ascertained	9	8	6	6	7	17	8	
	100	100	100	100	100	100	100	
Number of Cases...........	(78)	(324)	(113)	(138)	(197)	(60)	(468)	

*See Table IV.

TABLE XXIII

PERSPECTIVES TOWARD THE SCOPE OF GOVERNMENT BY SOCIAL CLASS
AND BY POLITICAL PARTY IDENTIFICATION

(In per cent)

| Perspectives | Social Class | | | | | | Total Sample | | |
| | Working Class | | Middle Class | | | | | | |
	Rep.	Dem.	Rep.	Dem.	Rep.	Ind.	Dem.		
Too much	9	2	22	4	17	13	2		
About right	58	43	60	48	58	40	45		
Not enough	29	53	15	44	22	37	50		
Don't know; not ascertained ...	4	2	3	4	3	10	3		
	100	100	100	100	100	100	100		
Number of Cases.............	(78)	(324)	(113)	(138)	(197)	(60)	(468)		

Although the difference is statistically significant, this can hardly be judged as a profound political divide.

The magnitude of the difference between Republicans and Democrats, however, is highlighted by demands for more action: 50 per cent for the Democrats as compared with 22 per cent of the Republicans, or a gap of almost 30 percentage points. It is this difference which supplies a meaningful basis for election competition. At the other end of the continuum, "The government is doing too much," the difference is smaller: Democrats 2 per cent as compared with 17 per cent of the Republicans, or a gap of 15 percentage points. Thus, the differences that do exist are not concentrated in that extreme of the continuum where they would be the most disruptive.

3. The most impressive confirmation of the hypothesis that differences in administrative perspective within parties exceed differences between parties emerged from an analysis of perspectives about the worth of government. While 49 per cent of the Democrats thought that the help and services that the public gets from the government is worth what it asks from the public, a similar percentage (51 per cent) of the Republicans were of this opinion (Table XXIV). Other opinions about the worth of government services were similarly distributed as between Democrats and Republicans. There seemed to be, however, a social class difference in the meaning of these

TABLE XXIV

PERSPECTIVES TOWARD THE WORTH OF GOVERNMENT SERVICES AND
POLITICAL PARTY IDENTIFICATION

(In per cent)

Perspectives	Republicans	Democrats
Government asks more......................	28	31
Government services are worth (equal to) burdens	51	49
Public gets more.........................	16	13
Don't know; not ascertained................	5	7
	100	100
Number of Cases..........................	(197)	(468)

responses. For example, the lower class person stressed the great importance of government as the *sole* and *fundamental* protector of economic and social rights:

Well there is a lot of unemployment and bad housing and misery in this country. You may not see it on the main streets, but come to back streets like ours and you will. Why we got neighbors that are all but down and out and we always are helping them. It ain't all their fault they ain't never had a chance and the government is all they got to look for help and it just ain't right that the government ain't doing more.

A similar orientation, of an almost desperate reliance on the public bureaucracy, often emerged for a lower class individual because of some particular assistance rendered by governmental action. A 21-year-old Negro auto worker from Oklahoma City spoke with real conviction when he said:

If it was not for the government we would have been out on the street. We were supposed to be out by the 15th of the month, but they let us stay longer. We had to appear in court and pay the rent and they let us stay until the 15th of the next month. We found a place. The city really helped us.

Among middle class persons, positive response to the worth of government seldom had the same saliency and urgency. It represented a more reasoned and detached opinion of a person who saw alternate pathways to life goals. For middle class persons, it was educational opportunities afforded by the state, rather than economic factors, which were able to evoke the same saliency. The educational system was regarded as a socializer of the youth, an enforcer of social norms, and a vehicle for upward mobility. An example is the 41-year-old housewife who said:

They should not allow kids to quit school at 17; should be compulsory to finish high school and in the last two years they should be able to pick up a trade and learn about it. To get anywhere in life, it's hard without an education. If men and women were better educated, the city and the country would be better.

Thus, the high consensus of persons with differing political party affiliations toward the symbols of administration in part is tempered by the differing meanings that social groups attribute to governmental services.

POTENTIALS FOR DISSENSUS

These data thus indicate that the compartmentalization of political research into "politics" and "administration," and the consequent neglect of "administration," is not an adequate basis for analyzing the spectrum of political behavior. Perspectives on public administration at the community level cannot be gauged from political party affiliation.

Moreover, these data call into question a major theme in current political behavior research. Political research into election and campaign ideology proceeds on a basis that defines "liberalism" as involving an extension of the scope of government, while "conservatism" involves an antigovernment and an antipublic bureaucracy orientation. This is the essence of the "left to right" formulation of the political process. This type of political analysis fails to specify the content of governmental activity which would threaten "liberal" goals. It fails also to specify the content of governmental activity which a "conservative" point of view requires. Shils, in his criticism of the monumental research effort of *The Authoritarian Personality*, holds also that the fascist-communist continuum of this and other political research implicitly makes use of such an orientation, without recognizing the unlimited pro-public bureaucracy emphasis of the extreme left and the extreme right.[3]

Many of the election surveys take the extension of the public bureaucracy as signifying liberal goals with the reverse signifying conservatism. In the 1952 surveys, only the intrusion of the Taft-Hartley labor issue led to a minor deviation from this pattern of analysis. By 1956 civil liberties, especially the McCarthy issue, and civil rights had impressed a series of

---

[3]Edward Shils, "Authoritarian: Right and Left," in *The Scope and Method of the Authoritarian Personality*, eds. R. Christie and M. Jahoda (Glencoe, Ill.: Free Press, 1954), pp. 24-49.

dilemmas on empirical studies of political ideology. The ideological content of political behavior can no longer be analyzed on the basis of a simple dichotomy of left to right, if left means more government and right less government.

A more comprehensive overview of the electorate implies that there are limitations to the extension and areas of administration for both conservatives and liberals. Full extension of the administrative authority is a goal of the radicals of the left and of the radicals of the right. Politics and administration based on consent implies that both conservatives and liberals, regardless of party identification, have conceptions—although differing ones—of the limitations of the scope and content of government. Despotic administration can be either despotism of the right or despotism of the left.

Standardized research procedures for distinguishing radicals of the right and radicals of the left which are applicable to mass populations have not yet been developed. Because this research focused so heavily on community based administration, contributions to this problem are indeed limited. Radicalism of the left and of the right involves broad national ideological and foreign policy considerations which were not investigated in this research. But it is clear that political party identification is hardly an index to fundamental orientations toward the symbols of administrative authority and, thereby, to liberal, conservative, or radical orientations. Public perspectives toward the administrative process, however, are clearly a direct aid in locating potential radicals of the right or of the left.

Within each party there is a group which rejects existing administrative authority and yet, simultaneously, demands an expansion of the scope of government in the area of social welfare functions. These are the persons who have a special potential for radicalism of the right or of the left. They are identifiable by cross tabulating the responses of acceptance-rejection of administrative performance against those given to the scope of government question. Although our measures and definitions are arbitrary these disaffected groups were thought to be, and were in fact, small. Using the extreme definition of the rejection of existing administrative authority (scale type 6) there were 70 persons, or 9 per cent of the total sample, who were classified in this potential radical category. When the broader definition of rejection was used (scale types 5 and 6) 128 persons, or 16 per cent of the sample, fell in this category. Table XXV presents these data arrayed by party identification with asterisks designating the potential radical groups. Because of the absence of validating research it can only be said that these subgroups have special potentials for radical political behavior. Further understanding of these groups depends upon an analysis of their attitudes toward civil liberties, internal communism, and foreign affairs.

Among the Republicans, 18 per cent were in the category of predominant rejection of metropolitan based administrative authority. Twenty-seven per cent of this subgroup demanded an expansion of the scope of government, nevertheless, and their perspective is not to be thought of as merely inconsistent. To the contrary, they are the potential radicals of the right. Their pseudoconservatism is inferable from their party affiliation. Their radicalism emerges from their simultaneous rejection of the public bureaucracy and their demands for its expansion, presumably on a different ideological basis. Those Democrats who fall into the predominant acceptance category and demand an expansion of government are likely not to be radicals because of their acceptance of the current system. Among the Democrats, however, 20 per cent fell in the group which predominantly rejected administrative symbols of authority. Sixty-two per cent of this subgroup call for an expansion of the scope of government. They are the potential radicals in the Democratic party. While some have a leftist orientation, others probably have a rightist outlook.

While we need to know much more about these potential radicals, there is reason to believe, from our data, that a good number of them have suffered downward social mobility. Some have experienced downward mobility to the lower middle class, others into the lower lower class. These are persons who no longer see a basic compatibility between their

TABLE XXV

PATTERNS OF POTENTIAL RADICALISM: ACCEPTANCE–REJECTION BY SCOPE OF GOVERNMENT AND BY PARTY IDENTIFICATION

(In per cent)

Perspectives	Party Identification					
	Republicans			Democrats		
	Predominate Acceptance	Intermediate	Predominate Rejection	Predominate Acceptance	Intermediate	Predominate Rejection
Too much..............	18	17	18	2	2	4
About right...........	63	54	55	53	45	31
Not enough...........	17	27	27*	43	52	62*
Not ascertained	2	2	...	2	1	3
	100	100	100	100	100	100
Number of cases	(84)	(66)	(33)	(173)	(173)	(86)

*Designates those groups which predominantly reject the existing pattern of administrative operations yet demand more government action in the social welfare area—the potential radicals of the right and left.

self-interest and the behavior of the public bureaucracy. These are persons for whom our four criteria of public administration based on consent has little validity and little meaning. But fortunately they constitute a most limited minority—at most, no more than ten per cent. Thus, some measure of fundamental consent with the metropolitan based bureaucracy is present for the public at large. Moreover, this consensus seems to imply that public officials are able to influence public perspectives toward the bureaucracy by means of official communications, public relations, and face-to-face contacts. The investigation of some essential aspects of the communications patterns of public officials with their publics was the final step in our research.

VII

COMMUNICATING TO THE PUBLIC:
BARRIERS AND CHANNELS

To COMPLETE the analysis of public perspectives toward the administrative process, we felt it necessary to augment our investigation of public perspective and contacts with administrative organizations. We felt it necessary to approach the administrator directly in order to ascertain how he viewed his clients and by what means he sought to communicate with them.[1] We were not seeking to determine which specific public perspective had been influenced by governmental communication—this was beyond our research design.

It was assumed, however, that public perspectives are conditioned by communications and communication is invariably a two-way process. What a person knows about public administration is in part a consequence of his self-interest. What a person knows about public administration is also, in part, a consequence of the public administrator's image of his clients and of the channels of communications he has to the citizenry. A clear understanding of his clients and of the citizenry is a requisite for his communicating effectively with them.

From our sample of government agencies, a sample of the personnel of three were selected—the public school system, unemployment compensation, and old-age and survivors insurance agencies. These three agencies have a mass clientele and are faced with complex and difficult problems in communicating with them and the general citizenry. They are all agencies with numerous operating units. Within the Detroit metropolitan area, the Michigan Employment Security Commission (MESC) has its administrative headquarters for the entire state and 14 of its 15 branch offices, while the U. S. Bureau of Old Age and Survivors Insurance (BOASI) operates five "field" offices. In the city of Detroit, the Board of Educa-

---

[1]For a full description of this aspect of the research see William Delany, "Bureaucrat and Citizen: A Study of Government Bureaucracies in a Metropolitan Setting" (unpublished Ph.D. dissertation, Univ. of Michigan, 1957).

tion (Bd of E) has a complete administrative staff and some 275 separately located schools. Within operating units like branch offices and schools there is a readily recognizable upper managerial level: office managers and assistant managers in MESC and BOASI units, and school principals, assistant principals, and vice-principals. For the three agencies a sample of 570 employees was selected, composed of 143 upper level and 427 lower level persons.[2] Data on agency employees' contact with clients and the general citizenry, as well as their knowledge of public perspective toward their agency, were collected by means of a paper-and-pencil questionnaire administered in the offices of the three agencies. Intensive informal interviews were also conducted with forty-four top managerial personnel, including those particularly concerned with public information and education activities.

Public officials have to communicate with different publics. They have to communicate with key group and association leaders, for the strategic political support of their agency depends upon these leaders. They have also the task of day-to-day communication with the agency's clients and with the citizenry at large. The patterns of communication between public officials and these publics, however, are fundamentally discontinuous and segmental. Each side has only a partial and all too fleeting contact and image of the other. These segmental contacts create powerful limits to communications between public agencies and their different publics. Additional limits

[2]In 1954, at the time of our field work, BOASI had 95 employees within metropolitan Detroit; MESC had 1,183; and for the city of Detroit the Board of Education had 13,316. In selecting respondents among these employees two criteria were used: (1) the employee's official position had to be in the upper managerial and administrative or lower operational level of the agency; (2) he had to be involved directly in the agency's performance of its day-to-day services to the population in the Detroit community. About half of the three agencies' employees (8,487) met these two criteria and form the universe of this special study. For the purpose of securing an adequate number of respondents for quantitative analysis, the entire universe was selected for the smallest staff, BOASI, and in the upper administrative and managerial level of MESC. For the lower operational level of MESC and for the Board of Education, two-stage probability sampling designs were used to select, first, branch offices or schools and, then, relevant employees within each of these. A high response rate of .92 was but one indication of the general interest and cooperativeness of our respondents.

to effective communication with these publics arise from the hierarchical organization within an agency and the segmental contacts that operate between upper and lower level personnel.[3]

COMMUNITY BARRIERS TO COMMUNICATION

The consequences of segmental contacts on effective communications in the metropolitan community have long been a topic of concern to the urban sociologist.[4] These segmental contacts—group and individual—and the impersonality that they imply are rooted in the structure of the metropolitan community. The size and density, the social stratification, and the rapid rate of social change of the metropolitan community are crucial factors that create problems of communication for public administrators.

Size and density

The size and density of the metropolitan community means that each important government agency has multiple operating units. Managerial civil servants in each operating unit must of necessity have limited lateral contact and communications. To prevent friction between operating units and to coordinate communications with organizational leaders, the agency's higher administration has had to establish "proper" channels. Managerial civil servants in these operating units tend to build up "proprietary" rights to service, and to communicate with particular firms, trade unions, newspapers, and radio stations and with clients in the area of "their" branch office or school. Continually, the personnel of one operating agency have to communicate with persons residing in the geographical district of another operating unit. The necessary rules for "clearing" with lateral operating units create communication barriers.

---

[3]An analysis of the internal barriers to communications in these three agencies is presented in Morris Janowitz and William Delany, "The Bureaucrat and the Public; A Study of Informational Perspective," *Administrative Science Quarterly*, II (September 1957), pp. 141-62.

[4]See especially Robert E. Park, *Human Communities: The City and Human Ecology* (Glencoe, Ill.: Free Press, 1952); and *Society: Collective Behavior, News and Opinion, Sociology and Modern Society* (Glencoe, Ill.: Free Press, 1955).

The size and density of the metropolitan community means, moreover, that the public official is likely to live in an area remote from the location of his particular operating unit. Branch managers, principals, and other key managerial officials of each operating unit, however, are expected to know personally those in their service areas with whom their agency deals— key organizational leaders, business and trade union representatives, and heads of voluntary associations.

Not only does the public official tend to live outside of the area, but some of the group and organizational leaders with whom he has contact live outside as well. Place of work and place of residence are indeed separated in the modern metropolis so that contacts tend to become limited to official agency duties. One administrator, who directs the operation of fourteen branch offices in metropolitan Detroit, summarized the problem and its implication when asked, "How much do the managers of the Detroit offices participate in the affairs of the area served by their office?"

Well, in the outstate offices [i.e., those outside metropolitan Detroit] the managers live in the communities which they are serving and participate actively in its affairs. The people they know in Lions or Chamber of Commerce outside the office are also the employers and claimants in the area they service. Thus, hardly anyone comes into one of the offices who isn't acquainted with someone in the office. This makes the work run a lot smoother. In Detroit, though, almost none of the managers actually live in the areas they service. For example, the manager at Mt. Clemens lives in Detroit. An exception is Dearborn. There the manager lives in the community and takes part in community activities . . . . But the Royal Oak manager doesn't live in Royal Oak but in Detroit. Most of the managers in Detroit are active in a number of civic and other organizations but the people they come to know socially are not usually those who they deal with each day as claimants, employers or trade union "Reps." As a result, from the point of view of the agency, such participation is not so important in Detroit. This makes dealing with the public in Detroit offices a lot more formal and increases the difficulties of our operations here.

The manager of another large MESC branch office underlined the same observation. He was born and raised in Wyandotte, has most of his intimate friends there, lives in Allen Park, and works in Detroit.

Isn't that typical of the metropolitan dweller? I belong to the Exchange Club in Wyandotte and am very active in their Chamber of Commerce. But the friends I make there don't help my job here in Detroit at all. In an outstate office, belonging to these groups would mean that I was getting to know socially employers and others who come into the office. . . . But even if I did belong to such groups here in downtown Detroit, which I don't, it wouldn't help much. You see, the people who work here in this area don't live here. They only work in the same area but live and belong to groups all over the metropolitan area. . . . [Therefore] I wouldn't say I know many of the management people well at all. Actually, I know the businessmen in Wyandotte better in a social way than the ones in my area here. Better, probably, than the manager of the office at Wyandotte.

Interestingly enough, our sample of metropolitan Detroit public employees was predominately recruited from the local environs, was longer resident locally than the rest of the metropolitan adult population, was highly identified subjectively with Detroit, and, finally, participated more extensively and intensively than the average middle class Detroiter in a great variety of voluntary associations. They had, in short, all the social characteristics that one would attribute to members of a civil service capable of contributing to the integration of an urban metropolitan community. Nevertheless, they were still party of the pattern of metropolitan life.

Social stratification

The patterns of social stratification in the urban metropolitan community determine the social prestige of the managerial public servant, influence his social access to groups and associational leaders, and thereby limit his communications potential. He is faced with a number of prestige barriers in his social contact with his community counterparts. Despite the rise in prestige of public employment, in the large metropolitan community such as Detroit the managerial civil servant has markedly lower social status than top businessmen, international labor union officials, large employers, and ranking persons in the mass media to whom he seeks access.

Repeatedly, members of our sample of managerial civil servants mentioned that noteworthy barriers to their contacts with business and management persons are the business "expense account," the expensive luncheon, the bar, and the golf club that often provide the setting for informal work contacts in the metropolis. One manager of a federal field office mentioned that a middle-sized firm employing one of his friends pays $1,000 a year for memberships in the O. . . . Country Club for the company's executives and salesmen. He had found out that one large auto manufacturer pays for forty employee memberships in that club alone. Reflecting on his comparatively lower income and the utter heresy of "expense accounts" in government employment, he said:

A government employee can't maintain social contacts with businessmen under such conditions. If you go along on golf games and such things and don't reciprocate invitations you're looked on as a "sponger." As a result, I stay away from all memberships and activities that my own budget won't handle. Today, for example, I was invited to a meeting of the E. . . . Club but refused. The lunch and especially the drinks you have to buy cost too much for me. I only go when I'm asked to address a meeting, then they usually pay for your lunch. . . .

With some emotion, he went on to talk about his contacts with the particular business and labor officials with whom he works in his service area:

I got to realize that I'm only a field office manager. If you face realities of life in a big city like Detroit you know that I have no dealings with really "big shots" in the big firms or union internationals. I couldn't mix with them if I wanted to because they all make at least five or six times my salary. . . . I don't belong to the real snooty clubs like the Detroit. . . . and the Detroit. . . . Even when it came to the E. . . . Club or the S. . . . Club, which are more my level and where I've already been invited, I can't afford it on the salary I make. Not that the dues are so steep. It's the lunches, the drinks, the tips and so on. . . .

Social status and lack of access to the metropolitan leadership serves to condition the civil servant's self-conceptions and limit his ability to make use of the mass media to project an image of government onto the public. This same federal official went on to say:

The things are a lot different here in a metropolitan area like Detroit than in a small town. I started out in this agency in a small town, as a manager in Smalltown, Ohio. In Smalltown, Ohio, I was known to everyone and knew all the "big shots" in the town. When I left, my name was on the front page of the paper. . . . Here, a field office manager gets to know people like those in charge of pension and retirement matters in the large firms . . . but naturally, not the executives who run the companies. In Smalltown the manager is considered one of the representatives of the Federal Government in the community, as Mr. Social Security. In Detroit, he is just another government employee, a sort of "glorified clerk" . . . .

Social stratification not only creates barriers to communication with metropolitan leadership groups but also separates the managerial civil servant of middle class orientation from those of his clients who are of the lower class. It was obvious, especially where the operating unit was in a Negro or working class area, that the middle class standards of the managing official himself created barriers to informal communications with unemployment or social security claimants and even with the local leaders of Negro and labor groups.[5] Again, these communication barriers associated with social stratification are probably not as great in small communities.

Rapid rate of social change

The rapid rate of social change in the metropolitan community contributes to segmental contacts and confounds communication problems. Industrial growth and the expansion of the urban community and suburbanization mean high rates of in-and-out migration and constant shifts in residence. The location and relocation of operating units is a common occur-

[5]Documentation of the middle class orientation of the school system and the negative consequences that this has for communications in lower class areas are available from other researches.

rence for both BOASI and MESC. As compared with the other barriers to agency communication, however, administrators were far from seeing shifts in population patterns and agency relocation as a serious problem. In part, they had learned to live with the disruptive consequences of shifts in populations. The clients likewise seemed to have learned to live with the disruption from the relocation of operating units. For example, one administrator commented:

You know as often as we have moved those God damned offices around we have never had a single beef from the public. Oh, once in a while someone will phone up to tell us he is out at the old office and wants to know where in hell we've moved it. But, personally I think you could move them anywhere and no one would complain. The American public is adjusted to change. As long as they can see that your new office is a better building, at a better location, nearer transportation and so on. They just accept the fact that we've made some improvement and don't question it.

More fundamental consequences of rapid social change arise from the need to modify continually the law and the legal basis on which these mass service agencies operate. Changes in the conditions of metropolitan life imply that new categories and new details have to be written into the law, even before the details of the existing law can be common knowledge. Many of the administrators emphasized these constant and often minor changes in the law as a crucial barrier to communication with the citizenry. In the words of one administrator speaking about his own agency:

The legislature has amended the law too often. They pass legislation which is not sound because they want to please too many interest groups who are interested in nothing but their own advantage. The result is a law which is a complex tissue of compromises. Many of our employees do not understand the law well enough.

As a result, the public agency is faced with the task of overcoming a lag in public information which is continually complicated by the introduction of new legislative changes. For example, the Michigan Employment Security Commission has developed a crude index of public information concerning its agency and program which it calls the "disqualification ratio." This is a ratio of unemployment compensation claims denied to all claims filed in a particular period of time. Before the major amendments to the law in 1948, the disqualification index was less than 8 per cent. In 1948 it rose to 16 per cent and then gradually declined over a period of years to 9 per cent. In each subsequent biannual year of legislature amendments the index showed a similar increase as in 1948, though not as marked or prolonged. Clearly, the complexity and frequent change of the law to meet new requirements is a basic barrier to public education.

INTERPERSONAL CONTACTS

To deal with these fundamental barriers to effective communications, government agencies in the metropolitan community must develop solutions which rest on their organizational resources. First, direct "face-to-face" contact with agency clients and with key private group and association leaders form the basic core of the public information program in these three agencies. Second, officially and unofficially, the mass media and mass devices are enlisted both by agency personnel and by private groups associated with these agencies. The resources available for the public relations function to these government agencies are indeed limited in a business enterprise system, and especially at the metropolitan community level of administration.

In any mass service agency, public information and public relations becomes an ongoing task of the entire agency. It is by means of a continuous flow of face-to-face, telephone, and written messages that information is disseminated to the mass clientele and to the association leaders linked to the agency.

The extent to which agency officials selected for study in these three agencies are involved in client contact can be seen from the extremely low percentage which did not have some direct interpersonal contact with agency clients or with the general citizenry during an "average" week. In all, about 96 per cent of these public employees from the three agencies reported that they had some such contact. (The percentage with no such official contact was for the BOASI 4.5 per cent; for MESC, 7.5 per cent; and for the Detroit Public school systems, 1.7 per cent.) Moreover, the amount of contact and interaction was high. During the average week, the modal employee had between 100 and 150 contacts.

In each agency, beyond direct operational contacts with clients, there are managerial and administrative assignments which carry the main responsibility for maintaining contact with private groups and association leaders. We found a variety of association and group leaders who communicate directly with the personnel in our three agencies. These contacts with group and association leaders link the public agency to the community power structure and to the general citizenry. These elected or appointed leaders represent a range from trade unions, management associations, veterans, business and civic groups like Rotary and Kiwanis to church, neighborhood, and youth groups.

Contact with association leaders, while extensive, was less widespread among agency staff than contact with agency clientele. Sixty-five per cent of the sample public employees have some contact in an average week with association leaders as compared with 96 per cent who have some contact with clients. As was to be expected, lower level employees tended to communicate more with the agency's individual clients, while upper level administrators had more frequent and diverse contacts with association leaders (Table XXVI). Fifteen per cent of the lower level employees had extensive contact with such leaders, while 36 per cent of upper level employees had contacts of this type. In addition, 21 per cent of upper level administrators communicated with leaders of four or more different kinds of associations while the figure for lower level was only 9 per cent. The concentration of these contacts with association leaders, however, can be judged when it is noted that only 6 per cent of our agency sample was involved with

TABLE XXVI

PROPORTION OF PUBLIC CONTACTS WITH ASSOCIATION LEADERS AND
ADMINISTRATIVE LEVEL

Per Cent of Leader Contact to All Contacts	Administrative Level			
	Lower Level		Upper Level	
	Number	Per Cent	Number	Per Cent
0 to 3 per cent...............	283	66	31	23
4 to 14 per cent..............	80	19	55	41
15 and over	64	15	47	36
Total...................	427	100	133	100

four or more diverse kinds of association or group leaders each week. Thus, while a limited amount of association contact work was spread throughout the agency, the bulk fell on a very small group who were in the upper level managerial category.

In tracing out the patterns of communication among upper level civil servants we soon discovered that we had to avoid a stereotype. Students of bureaucracy have placed much emphasis on letters, written rules, and paper work as essential traits conditioning bureaucratic behavior, especially its impersonality. Moreover, formal communications and impersonality are believed to be most concentrated at the upper levels of bureaucracy. In these three agencies, however, communications by telephone with clients, group representatives, and even the general public emerged as very important, especially for upper level administrators. It is true that we found upper level personnel tended to have less direct face-to-face communications than lower level personnel with clientele and the general citizenry. If direct communications includes the telephone as well as face-to-face contact, however, the difference between levels in directness of written communication with clients and the public declines sharply. (When direct communication was defined to include only face-to-face contacts, 79 per cent of lower level personnel dealt directly with the public in more than half of their public contacts as against 51 per cent of upper level administrators. When the definition of "direct" was broadened to include both face-to-face and telephone contacts, however, the relative percentages are 96 for upper and 94 for lower level personnel.) Thus, the public official relies heavily on the informality and flexibility of the telephone to expedite his daily routine, and modern bureaucracy has a much less formal system of communications than the ideal conception of it suggests.

It is striking to note the extent to which the association leaders involved in these face-to-face contacts with public officials were paid job holders rather than volunteers or elected associational officers. Group representation has come to be a professionalized occupation. Thus, for example, in approaching a mass social welfare agency like the BOASI or MESC, large firms, labor unions, veterans associations, and even service clubs rely on professional personnel for government contact work. The technical problems in social welfare require contact work by skilled specialists. This is less the case in the educational field, although here as well there were numerous professional staff people representing special interest groups. Thus, a large number of the public contacts of the upper level managerial civil servant in the metropolitan community seemed to be with these newer organizational professionals.

Most of the 44 top managerial civil servants who were interviewed agreed that interpersonal contacts in operational units constituted the main public information and education work of their agency. The success of over-the-counter "public relations" depends on the time allowed for office interviews and the skills and knowledge of personnel. Effective "community relations" depends upon the personnel resources available for out-of-office contacts. Inadequate funds and personnel prevent the development of effective office interviewing and community relations programs. In the operational units many of the top administrators interviewed were keenly aware of the problem and concerned to use their limited resources as effectively as possible. But the long-term trends in budget allocation have complicated their efforts and made them less and less effective.

In both the BOASI and MESC over the last decade increases in staff and administrative budget have not kept up with the growth of these programs. The school system is in a similar position. In fact, in the case of MESC the agency's staff has been decreasing in size without corresponding decreases in work load. Moreover, the quality of the interviewing skills of its branch offices is frequently diluted by hurriedly hired personnel demands due to large and sudden increases in work load from seasonal unemployment.

The pressure upon the staffs of most metropolitan branch offices of BOASI and MESC leads to a concern with expediting interviews and emphasis on the so-called "production" tasks. This means less time with each client and less effective interviews. In the words of one supervisor:

> Due to understaffing of the office, it has been necessary to conduct so-called guided interviews, to hold down the necessary time. Interviews would be much more enjoyable for the public and interviewers alike if it wasn't necessary to cut to a minimum interviewing time. This is undoubtedly the biggest deterrent to good public relations in this office at the present time.

Concern with the pressure of office production tasks in turn reduces public contact and informational activities outside of the office.

To begin with, budget and classification officers, although aware of and sympathetic to the need for giving consideration to outside contact and information activities, do not take bold steps in this area. Such activities are not easily measured and legislative pressures are against their inclusion. Because of the work pressure of office routines, even the meager staff time allocated for outside activities often cannot be used. Our interviews showed that many managerial civil servants are not merely "production minded." However, when faced with the choice of organizing and supervising either internal office interviewing or outside information activities prescribed for their roles, the majority are forced realistically to the first alternative. In one of the agencies, an office manager study done by the agency itself had concluded that most managers were, in fact, neglecting minimal outside information and education activities.

UTILIZATION OF MASS TECHNIQUES

Public information activities based on mass media techniques have hardly become an acceptable part of public administration in the metropolitan community. In fact, the pressures against the use of funds and personnel is so great that part of the public information function of these agencies has been transferred to private voluntary associations.

The difficulties which confront a public agency in its effort to obtain mass communications specialists are apparent in these three agencies. No agency can develop a mass communication program without the use of technical specialists. At the time of our interviews, BOASI had no public information technician in the Detroit metropolitan area. In fact, in 1952 the Congress eliminated the appropriation for a regional public information officer program, which had allocated one officer for the Michigan-Ohio office.

MESC does have one public information specialist in Detroit, an experienced newspaperman and part-time publisher of his own weekly newspaper in a small town in the Detroit metropolitan area. He plans the information and education for the entire agency and carries out most of the activities of the agency involving the mass media. His tasks include preparing and distributing press releases and magazine articles, writing radio and TV scripts, preparing speeches, posters, and exhibits, and performing other tasks normally assigned to a public relations specialist. Recently the budget reallocations eliminated his one full-time clerical assistant and, as he put it, "my staff has been reduced by 50 per cent." The Detroit Board of Education has a public information officer and a small but, apparently, adequate staff.

Despite these personnel limitations all three agencies seem to make resourceful use of the mass media. No administrator interviewed complained that the total public service time on radio or TV was inadequate, although clearly he was accepting the realities of the situation. Reliance on the metropolitan press seemed to be much less extensive, especially by the BOASI and MESC. These administrators were especially aware of the potentialities of the urban community press in residential and suburban areas. The same held true of the ethnic press.

The other devices of mass communications on which an adequate information program would have to be built were limited: films, slides, printed pamphlets, posters, charts, and window displays. On occasion, government pamphlets have been reprinted by business and labor groups for special distribution to employees or members.

Pressure against the development of a public information program arises out of the traditional fear that such activities constitute lobbying and should be prevented. The acceptance of a new government program does not bring with it acceptance of the belief that it should be empowered to inform the public of its implications. The opposition expresses itself first in legislative budget allocations. But special interest groups in the community are also constantly on the alert to the dangers of government publicity. As an upper level civil servant reported:

> Others in the community are also opposed to an extensive public information job. These are people in civic groups like the Chamber of Commerce and Rotary. Suppose your group is businessmen. When you go to give a talk at one of the civic groups on social security quite a few of them will stay away because they do not approve of making such talks. If you use a movie or slide or something like that to illustrate your remarks they don't like it and ask you "who is paying for all that stuff."

In a very real sense the scope and content of government is still evolving in the United States, especially in the areas of metropolitan government and in mass social welfare. Agencies are caught in a cross fire between interest groups opposing or sponsoring administrative legislation. Public officials seem to have to operate with enforced neutrality and with their expert advice hardly sought openly. This enforced neutrality limits their use of the mass media. To a point, neutrality of official and unofficial communications is essential if government agencies are to operate on the basis of consent. This means that official statements in the mass media and at public gatherings are carefully filtered to avoid controversial content. For example, a manager of one of the field offices of BOASI was asked to discuss, on a metropolitan newspaper's television program, the extension of coverage under social security then being enacted by Congress. Although the program operated without a fixed script it was necessary, of course, to discuss the questions and answers in advance. He agreed to speak without a script but insisted in being assured that:

They wouldn't put me on the spot by asking to defend or criticize the proposed legislation itself but just to keep it on an informational "how it will work" level.

The program director recognized the limits within which the civil servant must operate and the program stayed well within the studied boundaries of the currently noncontroversial.

In this process, administrative agency personnel tend to abandon leadership in public information affairs; they tend to give up the tasks of innovation and goal setting, even the technical responsibilities of drawing out the implications of their existing programs. The result is that public information becomes routine or tends to lose such of its interest and meaningfulness to citizen audiences.

Under these circumstances it is understandable that private groups enter into the field of public information in support of administrative agency programs. The activities of private groups become an important service to members and a force in molding the agency's programs. The co-optation of the public information function was to be found in all of the three agencies to varying degree and a full analysis of this process, although beyond this report, is essential for understanding the dynamics of the public administrator and his clients. For example, in the Detroit area, a great deal of effective public information on unemployment compensation and social security is disseminated by the labor unions and a great deal is also done by the employers. The struggle between labor and management involves the supplying of such information services as older conflicts fade and become transformed. The trade unions, especially the CIO-UAW, employ full-time technicians who are well informed on these laws and their administration. The unions develop elaborate information programs to reach their members and the information is presented dramatically and in such a manner as to meet the needs and interests of workers. Much the same is true of management, especially the large auto firms. In the education field, parent-teachers associations and religious and professional groups are active to the same ends.

In a democratic society, it is probably essential that significant aspects of public information for public agencies be carried on by voluntary associations and private groups. But danger arises when the public information function is weakened to the point of ineffectiveness or where the public bureaucracy is denied adequate freedom of action. Clearly, all of the agencies studied have developed an implied concept of administrative neutrality and the philosophy, so to speak, of a "third force" between conflicting groups. But to be an effective third force, agencies must have personnel for interpersonal and mass communications adequate to a positive role in areas where private groups do not and cannot operate.

VIII

ADMINISTRATIVE BEHAVIOR
AND DEMOCRATIC CONSENT

OUR OBJECTIVES were two-fold. First, we sought to describe public contact with government agencies in the metropolis and to investigate public knowledge and evaluations of the administrative process. We tried to uncover the correlates of these basic perspectives toward administrative authority. By analyzing the public's image of the administrative process we were studying by inference administrative "public relations" in its broadest context. Second, we sought to evaluate the extent to which these public perspectives were creating a political climate appropriate for administration based on consent. To this end we developed and applied four criteria with the hope that our analysis might be made relevant to the traditional interests of political theorists.

Our attention was on those administrative agencies which penetrate the daily routines of the metropolitan community. This arbitrarily neglects some crucial and controversial aspects of governmental administration. We believe, however, that the metropolitan community is the initial locus for the analysis of public administration and the public. The willingness and ability of the public to support the more remote aspects of administration depend in good measure on its more direct experiences with the organs of government.

OVERVIEW OF THE FINDINGS

It became apparent from our findings in the Detroit metropolitan community that political party affiliation was not a good index to fundamental differences in public perspectives toward the administrative process. Our assumption that these perspectives would not be sharply linked to partisan party politics was repeatedly confirmed. In fact, we found that an analysis of public perspectives toward administration is necessary to understand the nature of political consensus in the

101

United States. A national election demands that an individual commit himself on alternatives that involve remote decisions. The operations of metropolitan-based administrative agencies are diffuse and without the drama of partisan politics, to be sure. But these operations are direct extensions of personal and household reality for each citizen. They are activities of immediate involvement and concern, about which he can have more realistic judgments than about the more remote issues of national politics. Understandably, public perspectives toward these administrative processes, although hardly well informed, are relatively articulate and strikingly reflective.

These empirical data provide documentation of the rather pervasive acceptance of the current scope and performance of metropolitan-based administration. This is not to overlook either the small minority who object or the fact that specific operations of government may produce intense and outspoken criticism or rejection. Nor is this acceptance incompatible with the desire or even the demand for improvement. But our study did not probe willingness to support improvement. To some degree, the essential services of government are accepted simply because there is no alternative or because the public sees no possibility of alternatives. Our findings, however, underline the extent to which the new integrative functions of government, especially those connected with "service" government, have an impact on all strata throughout the social structure. All the various strata, not just the lower social groups in the metropolitan community, have developed a stake in and a reliance on these new functions of government. As a consequence, they contribute a basis for social and political consensus. For example, it should be recalled that only seven per cent of the population thought the scope of government welfare service was too broad or extensive.

These findings do not deny widespread ambivalent feelings towards the symbols of administrative authority. Ambivalence and reservation could be quickly mobilized by probing perspectives about the worth of government services and lack of principle mindedness among public servants. The fact that such negativism was less concentrated among young people may indicate a long-term trend. Generations which are growing up under the broadened scope of government are perhaps not so likely to hold the more negative orientations toward government authority historically attributed to the American public.

Also noteworthy was the finding that persons display a generalized syndrome of a tendency to accept or a tendency to reject the performance of administrative agencies. In other words, each member of the public seemed to address himself to the diffuse functions and organizations of metropolitan-based administration with some degree of self-consistency in his evaluation of its performance. Here our findings are merely compatible with the current assumptions of political behavior research which see political perspectives as being conditioned by underlying and persistent motivations. Along with the complex of perspectives concerning political partisanship we have identified another complex—that dealing with administrative authority.

For our second objective, that of evaluating the extent to which public perspectives were appropriate for administrative behavior based on consent, four categories—knowledge, self-interest redefined, principle mindedness, and prestige—formed the core of our analysis. A meaningful application of these categories would require trend data in order to establish the direction of social change. A meaningful application would also require comparative data on other nation states, such as Great Britain, to establish how much information, self-interest, principle mindedness, and prestige are required for democratic consent. For each perspective there is some optimum level, so that these four categories could be formulated into evaluative criteria and thereby constitute a bench mark for research.

First, the public failed to display extensive information about the practices of administration. The tests of the desired level of knowledge were indeed minimal. To avoid an over-intellectualized approach, a distinction was made between generalized knowledge and instrumental knowledge. *Generalized* knowledge deals with the understanding of the over-all working of an agency or a system of administration. *Instrumental* knowledge deals with the information essential to an individual about his rights and obligations concerning a specific agency. Clearly, instrumental knowledge was the crucial test, and the level of instrumental knowledge was somewhat higher than that of generalized knowledge. Contact—personal or familial— with a particular agency supplied a pragmatic means for overcoming social class and educational limitations on instrumental knowledge about that agency. But even contact did not necessarily produce a very well-informed citizenry.

The heart of the matter rests in the levels of ignorance that persist even after personal and family contact. Public administrators, public affairs leaders, and communications specialists must face the reality of a relatively uninformed citizenry. The majority of the population finds it difficult to translate its self-interest into an adequate level of understanding of key social welfare programs, such as social security. This is not a matter of lower class ignorance, for lack of knowledge penetrates deeply into the middle class. Our data revealed that widespread ignorance exists about other basic functions of government enterprise. But ignorance about key social welfare benefits is likely to have greater disruptive consequences for social stability than ignorance of other governmental activity since these programs are designed to deal directly with the sources of mass insecurity in the modern metropolitan community.

Nevertheless, lack of knowledge was not associated with a pervasive feeling that the public bureaucracy was thwarting personal self-interest. To the contrary, our second criterion— that the public bureaucracy must be seen as serving personal self-interest—was operative to a considerable degree. Self-interest must operate with built-in limitations. Therefore, as a check on the disruptive consequences of self-interested demands on the bureaucracy, the public must simultaneously acknowledge the bureaucracy's capacity to act as a neutral agent in resolving social conflicts.

In applying the criterion of self-interest, three different dimensions were investigated. One dimension assumed that for self-interest to be realized there would have to be a basic and essential acceptance, rather than rejection, of the current performance of the metropolitan-based bureaucracy. A pervasive or deep-seated antagonism against the organs of government—a crude anti-bureaucratic outlook—emerged as the orientation of only a small minority. The quantitative findings, although preliminary and perhaps arbitrary, fix the size of this group at between 10 and 15 per cent of the population.

A second dimension of self-interest assumed that agreement about the desired scope of government would be a manifestation of realized, rather than thwarted, self-interest. As pointed out above, opposition to the present scope of government, in social welfare for example, was also very limited; the transformation of government over the past two decades is now an accepted event. But this consensus should not be overinterpreted. Feelings of thwarted self-interest about the scope of government bureaucracy were lodged in varying degree among those persons who demanded an expansion of government administration at the metropolitan community level. About 40 per cent of the population has such an orientation. The demand for the expansion of governmental services was most concentrated in the lower class and less prestigeful social groups.

But it was on our third dimension of self-interest—the person's estimate of the economic worth of government—that disaffection emerged most sharply. No doubt it is a chronic and perhaps superficial popular reaction to decry high taxes and red tape in public administration. But the results of our probing of these topics are too convincing to dismiss the findings that a near majority feel hostile when these standards of administrative behavior are brought into question. These negative and hostile feelings were concentrated at the bottom of the social pyramid, where simultaneously the demands for more government administration predominate. It may well be that, in our mixed economy, the cost accounting and capital funding systems that public administration is developing as techniques of internal management control may assume new functions. These techniques may produce essential material by which public information programs can demonstrate to clients and public the economic worth of government operations.

The third criterion—that the public view the bureaucracy as being guided by principles—permits no simple evaluation since beliefs about morality in government emerged as more complex than we had anticipated. We did not uncover widespread belief in active corruption among public servants. The public, however, accepted without a sense of moral indignation the perceived importance of political pull in securing aid from administrative agencies. Political pull seemed to connote little more than those advantages of personal contact and acquaintanceships which were useful in dealing with the complexity and impersonality of large organizations. This seemed to be true of both public and private organizations. It was human, so to speak, to feel defensive in dealings with an impersonal government agency. Therefore, those persons who had intimate contacts with the public bureaucracy merely had desirable advantages. The growth and persistence of such a perspective, however, cannot be viewed as compatible with administration based on consent.

The fourth criterion, or requirement, dealt with the prestige of public employment. While we were not able to study in particular the prestige of the higher civil servants, there was a marked general improvement in public attitudes towards the civil servant since 1930. The trend emerged from a comparison of our data with those of Professor L. D. White collected over a quarter of a century ago. It seems hardly likely, however, that this enhanced prestige will rise to a level at which the prestige of the civil servant would endanger administration based on consent. Certainly, impressionistic observations about the higher civil servants' prestige seem to indicate that desired levels have not yet been reached. In the particular case of the military elite, leaving aside the role of the military hero as president, this key elite continues to have relatively limited prestige.

In summary, we believe that the categories of knowledge, self-interest, principle mindedness, and prestige describe consensus about the administrative process as it actually operates in the metropolitan community setting. Thus, to point out by means of these four public perspectives the extent to which administrative behavior rests on essential consent is not to ignore more precise specification of the vulnerabilities confronting our administrative system. With insufficient information, incomplete feelings of self-interest, and considerable indifference about principle mindedness consensus remains inadequate.

IMPLICATIONS FOR BALANCED ADMINISTRATION

It was our assumption that the evaluative concept of "balance" might serve to integrate these various types of public perspectives. From a functional point of view, the bureaucracy and the public are in a state of balance if the bureaucracy operates so as to prevent the creation of irreconcilable minorities. The resolution of emergent social and economic conflicts must be accomplished without resort to "despotic" or "subservient" behavior, for these are states of administrative imbalance.

For each type of imbalance two different varieties can be identified. First, the despotic bureaucracy can pursue its own goals to the exclusion of the goals which the public, through the political parties, is seeking to generate. Here the balance between organizational interests and electorate interests is disturbed in favor of organizational interests (despotic "self-serving"). Second, the despotic bureaucracy can pursue the goals of special interest groupings at the expense of accommodating itself to the needs of the larger society. Here, concern with special interests overshadows concern with general public interests (despotic "special interest"). The despotic bureaucracy tends to disregard public preference and demands. It is likely to resort to coercion and manipulation to maintain its power.

Both of these types of imbalance are reversed in the case of the unduly subservient bureaucracy. First, the subservient bureaucracy sacrifices essential organizational goals in the effort to satisfy electorate needs and requirements (subservient "self-destructive"). Second, the subservient bureaucracy fails to champion special interest needs because of opposing general social structure needs and goals (subservient "self-effacing"). This model can be presented in a simple paradigm:

	Administrative Imbalance "Despotic"	Administrative Balance "Consent"	Administrative Imbalance "Subservient"
Organizational Goals *versus* Public Interest Goals	"Self-serving" Administration Overemphasis on Organizational Goals		"Self-destructive" Administration Underemphasis on Organizational Goals
Special Interest Goals *versus* General Interest Goals	"Special Interest" Administration Overemphasis on Special Interest Goals		"Self-effacing" Administration Underemphasis on Special Interest Goals

We approached administrative behavior from an external point of view: what perspectives does the citizenry hold of public enterprise? How does this paradigm apply to the perspectives encountered in the Detroit metropolitan community? Strangely enough, the data we collected seem to reveal both elements of subservient and of despotic imbalance. On the axis of organizational versus public interest goals, whatever imbalance existed fell on the subservient side—on the side of the underemphasis of organizational goals ("self-destructive" administration). Preconditions for "self-destructive" administration exist because (1) the public bureaucracy is unable to contribute to the raising of public knowledge about its operations; (2) the public bureaucracy is unable to develop administrative practices which would work against the public's view of the inevitability of political pull and the absence of principle mindedness; and (3) the public bureaucracy does not command sufficient prestige to achieve its organizational goals. On the axis of special interest versus public interest goals, the evidence on public perspectives points in the direction of despotic imbalance. Here, in particular, are the feelings of the lower income and lesser prestige groups that the public bureaucracy does not sufficiently serve their self-interest.

These imbalances toward subservient behavior and toward despotic behavior do not cancel themselves out to produce balanced administration. The result, to the contrary, is strain and uncertainty. The result is the unstable position of the public servant in United States society in which his behavior is defensive and yet seemingly, at times, arbitrary in the exercise of power. Is this not to be expected when the role of governmental enterprise is undergoing rapid change and the rules for judging performance not yet clearly established?

Foreign observers have repeatedly commented on the uneasiness with which government administrative authority is exercised in the United States. This is the result not only of the organization of public administration in the United States, but also of the ambivalent public perspectives toward administrative authority in our culture and society. National differences in perspectives toward administrative authority rest on the most basic differences in cultural and social systems. Understanding of these processes emerges by means of comparative and cross-societal analysis. Thus, Margaret Mead, in her analysis of *Soviet Attitudes Toward Authority*,[1] seeks to demonstrate that Soviet administration is not an authoritarian system merely because of the arbitrary and brutal sanctions it employs. Like our model, she assumes that the administrative process rests on the dynamics of public perspectives toward authority which expect the governmental apparatus to be extremist and repressive. Soviet attitudes toward authority are

[1]Margaret Mead, *Soviet Attitudes Toward Authority*; An Interdisciplinary Approach to Problems of Soviet Character (New York: McGraw-Hill, 1951).

conditioned by contemporary administrative practices, but they are rooted in historical Russian traditions.

Analyzing administrative behavior from the point of view of public perspectives—from the external standpoint—is almost certain to result in policy considerations pointing to the need for public informational programs. The application of our four criteria clarify, perhaps, the goals for such efforts. It is not merely a task of disseminating more information. Present efforts to increase the level of public knowledge, to project a clear image of the worth of government, and to raise the prestige of public service seem inadequate. They seem to be without focus as well.

The results of this study, if they have any relevance of application, are that public perspectives toward metropolitan-based administration are much more favorable than the opinions reflected in the contents of the mass media. The media find it difficult to emphasize the routine achievements of the public bureaucracy. They seem required to focus on the crisis situation and on the dramatic. Whatever limitations the public has in understanding the processes of government, in wide areas the routine performance of metropolitan-based administrative agencies supplies a means for checking many of the criticisms levelled at the public bureaucracy in the mass media. In any case, the consensus about metropolitan-based government is such as to imply that public information programs, if adequately designed, will not encounter overwhelmingly negative barriers.

Scarcity of administrative resources is the limiting factor. Government agencies are not permitted to develop informational staffs to fill the gaps between hierarchical levels and between agency personnel and the public. Civil service managerial personnel and facilities in the agencies studied impressed us as generally inadequate for effective "community relations" programs. Given their limited resources, we were impressed however with the ingenuity used by personnel to solve these problems. The upper levels of the agencies were aware of their enforced neutrality among the competing power groups in the metropolitan community. They knew that as community-based agencies they had to make use of the imperfect, though extensive, social consensus in the community to develop their informational activities. This meant that, in large part, the task of disseminating information about their programs was assigned to voluntary associations and economic groups—business, labor, and special interest. The administrators were fully aware of the local community press and utilized it because of its emphasis on consensus in residential and suburban communities. The solutions they had to find were obviously inadequate but, just as noteworthy here, they were realistic. The problems of governmental communications with the metropolitan community will remain unsolved until organizational resources are placed at the disposal of administrative agencies.

Only by thinking in such long-range terms can progress be hoped for in the presentation of metropolitan-based government in the mass media. Perhaps the findings of this study will supply to the policy makers of the mass media a reasoned argument that a positive rather than a negative approach to the public information requirement of metropolitan-based government is very much in order. In short, leadership from the mass media is possible since the public is already prepared for leadership.

Informational efforts need also to encompass the civil servants themselves. The self-conceptions that civil servants have of themselves are more negative than those accorded them by the public. One agency executive when presented with our findings made use of these data in order to develop a more realistic and more favorable self-conception among the members of his agency. A realistic understanding of the position of the civil servant in the metropolitan community—based on research findings—can only serve to enhance the drive toward professionalization and to overcome feelings of self-depreciation.

In the search for information channels to the public, no possibility should be overlooked. For the so-called unreachables—those whose self-interest does not guide them to realistic concerns or who are unaffiliated or at least non-participators in associational life—for them, their children and the public educational system remain as a possible mass communication channel. In this respect, the observation of many social scientists that children must and do help socialize and educate their parents in modern society assumes new and specific meaning.

One cannot avoid the comparison between public bureaucracies and private ones. Our observations of the informational gaps between administrative staffs and their clients are probably more applicable to public agencies than to large-scale private corporations. The danger of competition and the prospect of loss of clients to competitors leads management to create special organizations to collect information about clients. Market research and consumer analysis is an accepted tool of business management. The lack of a market research orientation towards the clientele of public agencies is not a result of a lack of interest among public administrators. Resources are limited and social research on the clients of public agencies is too often considered lobbying. In the course of our research we encountered again and again the administrator's desire to have the type of data we were collecting. Until public agencies are able to develop support for such research, university-based work will have to be a temporary stopgap.

To speak of the need for positive public information programs does not mean that planning and development should exclusively be preoccupied with the mass media and with mass channels. Our findings emphasize the pervasive character of "over-the-counter" activities and of the face-to-face contacts with administrative personnel. Scarcity of resources is at work here just as in the case of the bureaucracy's utilization of mass media. In a sense, the scarcity of resources is even more disruptive since inadequate mass media programs represent administrative limitations, but poorly trained and overworked contact personnel are a positive liability. To be concerned with the improvement here is not to overlook the observation that, as of the present time, a person's contact with public agencies is less important in fashioning perspectives than is his position in the social structure. Thus, we are saying that a person's perspective toward an agency is more a function of what he judges the agency contributes to his self-interest and less a function of the way in which the agency presents itself to him.

Yet it would be most misleading and incomplete if the policy implications of this research were exclusively directed to public relations and public information. This study sought to extend beyond concerns with direct internal management of public administration. It was a basic assumption that administrative behavior needs to be analyzed in the context of politics and the political process. The development of the public bureaucracy is in the last resort "politic" in the common sense meaning of the word. In planning the strategy of legislative reform, in developing and recruiting a civil service and in guaranteeing its accountability political issues are at stake.

We have preliminarily identified those persons who believe that their self-interest fundamentally clashes with the current performance of the public bureaucracy. These are the individuals who see no possibility of modifying the system to meet their basic needs. These are the persons who demonstrate their potential for dissensus and radicalism. Fortunately, their numbers are rather small. Only long-term political and social change is likely to influence them; they are already, so to speak, outside the democratic body politic.

It is fashionable to decry administrative reliance on voluntary associations as private co-optation of public functions. One just cannot overlook the findings of social science research in the field of communication which highlight the advantages of voluntary associations as more efficient and effective means of communication to their members than are the generalized mass vehicles. There are undoubtedly dangers when public information programs of governmental enterprise must rest exclusively on voluntary associations. But without a multiplicity of voluntary association outlets and resources a pluralistic society is impossible. The alternative would be co-optation of information activities by the political parties; and there seems to be no reasons why such an arrangement would necessarily be advantageous.

In any case, an important share of the task of informing the public will continue to fall on the general mass media over which the processes of government have no direct control. What is required in order that the mass media policy makers accept the strategic responsibility for implementing the information requirements of metropolitan-based administration? It is striking to observe that wide sections of the mass media at the close of World War II accepted the responsibility of presenting religious and ethnic problems in a manner compatible with political democracy. The task here, as in the case of the presentation of metropolitan-based government, is the interpretive background. The mass media accepted this responsibility once it became abundantly apparent that new forms of social consensus were developing in the United States. Once wide sectors of the mass media accepted this responsibility of presenting religious and minority groups in a meaningful context, the strategic results in public enlightenment over a decade have been noteworthy.

We have also preliminarily identified those persons who display feelings of thwarted self-interest, but who are still positively disposed to the processes of political change and in a fundamental sense still are in consensus. For these individuals the danger seems to rest on their reliance on "economic" criteria for judging the worth of government. There can be no doubt that in some areas, the public bureaucracy can justify its productivity and enterprise more effectively to them by demonstrating the dollar worth of services it renders. But in the last resort, many of the services of government are unique and are difficult to translate into the language of the market place. The justification of the legitimate goals of administration is a political task. It involves the election process and the deliberation of the legislature. It is not the primary or ultimate task of the public administrator to justify his own activities; this is the task of the politician and the public affairs leader—both on the national and on the metropolitan community level.

APPENDIX A. SAMPLING TECHNIQUE[1]

THE FIRST step was to define the area to be included in the survey. For the purpose of the annual surveys conducted by the Detroit Area Study, the Detroit area has been defined as those parts of Wayne, Macomb, and Oakland counties which are divided into census tracts. The availability of relatively inexpensive and up-to-date population data for this area in the U.S. Census Reports was an important consideration in arriving at this definition.

The tracted area does not coincide exactly with the official Detroit Standard Metropolitan Area used by the U.S. Census Bureau. The Census S.M.A. includes *all* of the three counties. Population estimates for the subdivisions in the excluded, non-tracted area are considerably more difficult to secure, and the cost per interview in this area rises in general with the distance from the center of the City of Detroit. The Detroit area, as defined for the purpose of this study, includes approximately 89 per cent of the total population of the three counties. The inclusion of the remaining 11 per cent of the population, which is widely distributed in the outlying portion of the official Census S.M.A., did not seem warranted in view of the added cost of sampling and administration of field work in this area.

The next step was to define a sampling unit so that a known probability of selection can be assigned. Although we were ultimately interested in obtaining a sample of individuals to be interviewed, private dwelling units, rather than individuals, were given equal probability of selection. The technical problem of listing to provide a frame for the selection of the sample is more easily met with this designation.[2] An individual had a chance of being selected into the sample only if he were attached to a dwelling unit. Institutions and hotels, as well as non-dwelling structures, were excluded. Since only a small

---

[1]Adapted from Detroit Area Study Report M-19 by John Takeshita, "Selection of a Sample of Dwelling Units for the Detroit Area Study, 1954-55."

[2]For a full description of this procedure see: Leslie Kish, "A Procedure for Objective Respondent Selection within the Households," *Journal of American Statistical Association*, XLIV (September 1949), pp. 380-87.

proportion of people live in these places, the additional cost involved in listing and making selections did not warrant their inclusions. The initial decision on the approximate number of dwelling units to be included in the sample depends on consideration of the objectives, of the costs, and of the procedures of the survey. For the Detroit Area Study surveys, a sample of 900 dwelling units was deemed adequate. Since the tracted portion of the Detroit Metropolitan Area was estimated to have about 800,000 dwelling units in 1951, the basic sampling rate was fixed at about one in 900 (800,000 ÷ 900). This meant that every private dwelling unit in the area was given one chance in 900 of being selected.

This over-all rate was used for the 1953-54 sample, but adjustment was made in assigning measures of population size to sampling units at the various stages of selection to reflect the estimated growth since 1951. The procedure for selection is determined on the basis of the considerations of the study objectives and of the available resources. Briefly, the selection procedure for the Detroit Area Study involved the selection of primary sampling units in the form of census tracts, the selection of sample blocks within the selected tracts, and the listing in these blocks of dwelling units from which the final sample was drawn. The 1953-54 sample of 900 dwelling units came from about 300 blocks with clusters of three to four blocks from each selected census tract. The blocks were designed to yield a cluster of three dwelling units each. This design is, in general, an acceptable compromise between two factors with conflicting effects on the efficiency of the sample design. The greater the spread of the sample the more accurately will it represent the diverse elements of the population. But such a sample will result in greater cost per interview than one spread less widely.

The sampling procedure that was used in the selection of dwelling units in the Detroit area is technically known as *multistage area sampling*.[3] It was an *area sample* because the

<hr />

[3]For a more complete discussion of the procedure for multistage area sampling see: Leslie Kish, "A Two-Stage Sample of a City," *American Sociological Review*, XVII (December 1952), pp. 761-69.

procedure involved the identification of dwelling units within area segments (census tracts and blocks), and the selection of dwelling units was dependent upon a prior selection of these segments. It was a *multistage sample* because the procedure involved the selection of sampling units in several stages. At the first stage, census tracts were selected from among all such tracts in the Detroit metropolitan area. At the second stage, sample blocks were selected from among all the blocks within the tracts selected in the previous stage. At the third or final stage, dwelling units were selected from among those located within the sample blocks.

This type of sample is called a *probability sample* because the probability of selection of every dwelling unit is known. That probability (1 in 900 in the original DAS sample design) is the product of the probabilities of selecting the tract, of selecting the block, and of selecting the dwelling unit within the block.

At each of the three stages of selection the widely used method of *systematic sampling* was employed. At the first stage, all the tracts in the area were placed in a systematic order and a measure of size, based on an estimate of the population, was assigned to each tract. Then a sampling interval (K) was applied after choosing a random starting number from one to K. The random start and every Kth number thereafter determined the selection of the particular census tracts as the primary sampling units for this design. By the same type of procedure, blocks were selected within each primary sampling unit and dwelling units within the sample blocks.

A procedure used for increasing the precision of the sample is called *stratification*. It involves the arranging of the units being sampled into relatively homogeneous groups, or strata, and carrying through the selection within each of the strata so defined. In the present case, the information provided in the 1951 publication, "Administrative and Planning Areas in Metropolitan Detroit," by the Council of Social Agencies of Metropolitan Detroit, was used for the stratification of the first stage units.

The census tracts were grouped into 44 areas whose boundaries were established on the basis of the following kinds of criteria: (*a*) size of the population and the area, (*b*) homogeneous population characteristics, (*c*) location of community facilities, (*d*) physical barriers, (*e*) multiples of census tracts, and (*f*) civil divisions. But instead of making allocations to each of these areas, as is the usual procedure when stratification is utilized, a systematic selection was made by applying a constant interval to the list of census tracts which were arranged geographically according to these areas. This procedure, in effect, produced a stratified sample of census tracts. A similar result was obtained in the selection of blocks, for within each of the selected census tracts a systematic selection was made from among the constituent blocks. These blocks were given consecutive numbers which followed a serpentine order on a map.

The extent to which this selection procedure yields a sample that reflects the diverse elements of the population in regard to the variables in which the study is interested measures the effectiveness of stratification that is implicit in the ordering and selection scheme used. Stratification increases the precision of the sample only insofar as the variables used in grouping the census tracts are correlated with the characteristics to be measured by the survey and to the extent that it assures the selection of a sample that reflects the diversity of the population with respect to these characteristics.

Clustering is a method often used to reduce the cost of administering the field work by cutting down the expense of travel from address to address. The sample so selected, however, loses some of the precision it may have gained by stratification. The loss in precision is a function of the degree of homogeneity of the units forming the cluster. In the present design, clustering occurred at two stages—in the selection of blocks within the primary sampling units and in the selection of dwelling units within the sample blocks. Instead of distributing the sample blocks over the entire tracted area of greater Detroit, they were concentrated within a limited number of census tracts. Similarly, instead of spreading the sample of dwelling units over as many blocks as the size of the sample, a cluster of three dwellings per block was selected only in those blocks already selected at the second stage.

The loss in precision from clustering was offset in some measure in the present study by selecting the sample blocks with probabilities proportional to the estimates of the number of dwelling units they respectively contained. This compensation was deemed desirable when clusters of equal size were selected from blocks which contained a variable number of dwelling units. As a matter of fact, if blocks were not selected with probabilities proportional to size, the stated aim of equal probability for all the dwelling units in the area would have been violated.

One way of checking the general adequacy of our sample selection and interviewing is to compare our findings with those obtained from other sources where that is possible.

Although our survey was made three years after the 1950 U. S. Census, it is possible to compare some of our findings with census data. Where comparisons are made with census data for the Detroit Metropolitan Area, it should be noted that the Detroit Standard Metropolitan Area, as defined by the census, covers a somewhat larger area and population than our Detroit Metropolitan Area.

Table XXVII shows that the Detroit Area Study data on number of persons per dwelling unit correspond very closely to those of the census.

Table XXVIII indicates a close correspondence between our findings and the U. S. Census report on home tenure, that is,

TABLE XXVII

NUMBER OF PERSONS IN DWELLING UNIT FOR THE DETROIT METROPOLITAN AREA: COMPARISON OF FINDINGS OF U. S. CENSUS (1950) AND DETROIT AREA STUDY (1953 AND 1954)

(In per cent)

Persons in Dwelling Unit	U. S. Census 1950	Detroit Area Study 1953	Detroit Area Study 1954
1	6	7	6
2	28	28	28
3	24	24	21
4	20	22	21
5	12	9	13
6	6	5	7
7 or more	5	5	4
Total	100	100	100

the proportion of dwelling units owner-occupied and the proportion renter-occupied.

The U. S. Census found that 16 per cent of the population of Detroit was nonwhite in 1950. This compares with a finding of 15 per cent nonwhite in the Detroit Area Study for 1953 and 14 per cent for the 1954 survey.

Table XXIX shows a close correspondence of occupational distributions for the U. S. Census and the Detroit Area Study.

TABLE XXVIII

TENURE STATUS FOR OCCUPIED DWELLING UNITS FOR DETROIT AREA: COMPARISON OF FINDINGS OF U. S. CENSUS (1950) AND DETROIT AREA STUDY (1953 AND 1954)

(In per cent)

Tenure Status	U. S. Census 1950	Detroit Area Study	
		1953	1954
Owner occupied	65	65	68
Renter occupied	35	35	32
Total......................	100	100	100

TABLE XXIX

MAJOR OCCUPATION GROUP FOR WORKERS IN THE DETROIT AREA: COMPARISON OF FINDINGS OF THE U. S. CENSUS (1950) AND DETROIT AREA STUDY (1953 AND 1954)*

(In per cent)

Major Occupation Group	U. S. Census 1950	Detroit Area Study	
		1953	1954
Professional, technical and kindred workers	9	9	9
Manager, officials, and proprietors ...	9	10	11
Clerical, sales and kindred workers ...	22	18	19
Craftsmen, foremen and kindred workers	19	20	23
Operatives and kindred workers	27	29	23
Service workers, including private household	9	9	10
Laborers	5	4	4
Not reported	1	1	1
Total......................	100	100	100

*The data from the U. S. Census are for employed persons 14 years of age or older. The data from the Detroit Area Study are for persons in the labor force, 21 years of age or older.

APPENDIX B. THE INTERVIEW SITUATION

1. INTRODUCTION FOR INTERVIEWERS

A BRIEF statement of the purposes of the study was sent in a letter to the head of the household at each address in the sample. A copy of the letter appears below:

Dear Head of Household:

Every year the Detroit Area Study of the University of Michigan conducts a public-opinion survey and a sample population census throughout the Detroit Area. The purpose is to get an accurate picture of the characteristics of the people in Detroit and how they feel about some important problems.

Your house has turned up as one of 800 addresses selected by chance in order to give us an accurate cross-section of the Detroit Area.

At each address we will want to interview one person. We do not know anyone's name and will not ask for it. All interviews are entirely confidential. They are combined in a statistical report and no person is identified.

In order that this cross-section sample be accurate, we cannot make substitutions, but we ask our interviewers to be sure to talk with a certain member of the household at each of the selected addresses. An interviewer, carrying proper identification, will call at your home sometime during the months of January, February, or March. I feel sure that the member of your household interviewed will find this visit interesting and worthwhile.

The study has as its Citizens Advisory Committee a group of Detroit community leaders. Their names are listed in the enclosed folder, "Why Ask Me?," which will answer many questions about the study. If you have any other questions, our interviewers will be glad to answer them.

Sincerely,
Morris Axelrod (signed)
Director

The following instructions were issued to the interviewing staff on how to introduce themselves:

The introduction to this study should not pose any special or unusual problems. The subject-matter of the interview is of interest to everyone and gives people a chance to talk about the things in which they are interested and the things which affect their daily lives.

The findings of this study will be made available to interested people in government, in universities, in business, in labor, and to other civic leaders. A number of such civic leaders—religious, labor, and business—have indicated an interest in results and their great usefulness to them.

A suggested introduction is: "My name is _____ (*show your identification card*) and I'm from the Detroit Area Study of the University of Michigan. You probably received our letter about the survey we are making of community attitudes in and around Detroit. We are interviewing a cross-section of people in the Detroit area, and this is one of the addresses selected where I am to stop and talk to someone living here. Of course, the interviews are strictly anonymous—we don't want anyone's name." This is only one possible way of phrasing the introduction. Make whatever changes in this introduction you think necessary and helpful in your own case.

After your initial introduction at the door, you should proceed saying something like this: "Before I know to whom to speak here, I need to know how many persons twenty-one years of age and over live here. The reason for this is that we want to get a cross-section of the population, and we want to be sure that we don't talk only to men, or only to women, or to people all about the same age, so each place I go, I use this chart here which picks out the exact person I'm supposed to talk to, and makes sure that we get an accurate survey." You then list on the face sheet the occupants of the household (by relationship to the head of the household, *not* by name).

If the respondent is other than the first person to whom you speak, you will have to introduce yourself again, this time to the selected respondent, modifying the introduction according to the circumstances.

Sometimes you may find it necessary or desirable to identify yourself again at the end of the interview, and again show your card. Do this also if someone comes in while you are conducting an interview if it seems necessary.

2. THE INTERVIEW SCHEDULE

A COMMUNITY STUDY

1. Some people like the Detroit Area as a place to live; some people don't. What things do you think are good about living in the Detroit Area?

2. What things do you think are not good about living in the Detroit Area?

Now we would like to get some of your ideas about what sort of job the government is doing. First, let's start with the city.

3. Do you think the (*name of local community*) officials and bureaus are doing a:
   POOR,   FAIR,   GOOD,   or VERY GOOD   job?

4. What about the (*name of county*) county government—do you think the county officials and bureaus are doing a:
   POOR,   FAIR,   GOOD,   or VERY GOOD   job?

5. And the state government—do you think the state officials and bureaus are doing a:
   POOR,   FAIR,   GOOD,   or VERY GOOD   job?

6. How do you feel about the public schools in (*community name*)?
6a. Why is that?

7. Suppose you found out that a teacher was treating a child of yours unfairly, could you do anything about it?

8. Do you happen to know how the people on the Board of Education get their jobs?

9. Have you had any dealings at all with the Michigan Employment Security Office? That's the state office that handles unemployment insurance and helps people get jobs.
(*If yes*) 9a. What about?

10. Has anyone in your family (aside from yourself) ever received unemployment payments?

11. Do you know how many weekly checks a person can get under unemployment insurance?

12. Do you think unemployment insurance is good for the country?
12a. Why?

Let's talk about another important government agency:

13. Are you, or is anyone in your immediate family, now registered with selective service? (*If explanation needed, add:* for the draft?)

14. Do you think that the draft board handles deferments fairly here in the Detroit Area?

15. If someone isn't satisfied with how his draft board has classified him, could he try to change it?
    (*If yes*)   15a. What could he do?

16. In general, if you had a problem to take up with a government bureau, would you do it yourself, or do you think you would be better off if you got the help of some person or organization? (*If get outside help*)   16a. Who would that be?

17. In general, would you say that your dealings with public employees were:
    POOR,   FAIR,   GOOD,   or VERY GOOD?

18. Some people think political pull plays an important part in whether the government will help a private citizen with some problems he has; other people don't think so. In your opinion, does political pull play an important part in whether the government will help a private citizen?

19. Many people use the words "red tape" to describe their experiences with government. Could you tell me what you think they mean by red tape?
    19a. Could you give me an example of that from your personal experience?

20. As we know, all government bureaus have some red tape. On the whole, how much of it do you feel is really necessary?
    a) Most   *c*) Less than half
    b) More than half   *d*) None

21. If the pay were the same, would you prefer to work for the United States Government or for a private firm?
    21a. Why?

22. Would you say that generally you get more courteous attention in dealing with city employees than in dealing with employees of big companies?

23. We'd like to know what people think of government jobs and government workers. If these jobs (*hand card to R*) are about the same in kind of work, pay, and so forth, which have the most prestige?

    a) a stenographer in a life insurance company, or
       a stenographer in the city tax assessor's office
    b) an accountant in the Detroit Department of Public Works, or
       an accountant in a private accounting firm
    c) a night watchman in a bank, or
       a night watchman in the City Hall
    d) a doctor in the Detroit Receiving Hospital, or
       a doctor who is on the staff of a private hospital

24. How many of the high government officials would you say are probably dishonest and corrupt—many of them, just a few, or none at all?

25. We know that there are many reasons why people don't get to vote in elections. Could you tell me whether you voted in these elections:

    25*a*. First, the last local election? (*In Detroit, add:* That would be in November, when Lincoln ran against Cobo.)
    25*b*. Now, the presidential election—did you vote then?
       (*If R is under 25, omit question 25c.*)
       25*c*. How about the 1948 presidential election when Truman ran against Dewey?

26. Generally speaking, do you consider yourself a Republican or a Democrat?
    (*If R says "independent"*) 26*a*. Do you think of yourself as closer to the Republican or closer to the Democratic Party?

27. Have you ever helped campaign for a party or candidate during an election—like putting in time or contributing money?

28. Some people think the national government should do more in trying to deal with such problems as unemployment, education, housing, and so on. Others think that the government is already doing too much. On the whole, would you say that what the government has done has been *about right*, *too much*, or *not enough?*
    28*a*. How do you mean?

29. There is a lot of talk these days about a national health insurance plan to help people with their medical bills. Who do you think should run such a plan?
    a) Non-profit agencies, or
    b) The government, or
    c) People should take care of their own medical bills.

30. In general, do you think there is any corruption in the collection of taxes?

31. Do you happen to know how much money a person had to make last year before he has to file an income tax return this March 15?

32. What benefits does social security entitle you to?
    32a. Any others?

33. Do any members of your family receive social security benefits? (*If yes*) 33a. What kinds?

34. (*If R is under 65*)   a): How well do you think social security benefits will meet your needs when you retire?

    If R is 65 or over)   b): How well do social security benefits meet your needs?

Government offices are always interested in knowing whether people understand how they work.

35. Is it correct that if a person is 65 and wants to collect his government old-age insurance, he can't if he has any private insurance?

36. There is a plan to change social security so that everybody over 65 would get the same pension regardless of whether they have been paying social security tax. What do you think of this idea?

37. Here is a list of some agencies. Would you look at it and tell me which of these you have had any dealings with in the past year?
    a) Public Library
    b) Public Transportation System
    c) Tax Assessor's Office
    d) Street and Alley Cleaning

38. (*Ask for each agency contacted*): What sort of a job did you feel they were doing?

39. What about the County Sheriff's Department—what kind of a job are they doing?
    POOR,   FAIR,   GOOD,   VERY GOOD

40. And the State Police—how good a job are they doing?
    POOR,   FAIR,   GOOD,   VERY GOOD

41. What kind of a job would you say the (*name of local community*) police are doing?
    POOR,   FAIR,   GOOD,   VERY GOOD

42. In your opinion, what is the most important job that the (*community name*) police do?

43. Have you ever had to get in touch with the police for help about a problem?

44. As some people see it, there are different kinds of things the government has to do. The government has to provide help for people. The government also has to make people carry their share of the burdens and make sacrifices. Which one of these statements comes closest to your own opinion about this:

    a) The help and services that the public gets from the government is worth what it asks from the public.

    b) The government asks more from the public than it gives in help and services.

    c) The public gets more from the government than it gives the government.

45. Some people feel that they pay more taxes than they should, considering what they get from the government. How do you feel about this?

    45a. Why?

46. Of all the taxes paid to the government in Washington, what portion would you say is being used to pay for national defense and foreign aid:

    a) Two-thirds or more

    b) About one-half

    c) A third or less

47. Now I'd like to read some of the kinds of things people tell me when I interview them and to ask you whether you agree or disagree with them. I'll read them one at a time and you tell me whether you *strongly agree, agree, disagree,* or *strongly disagree:*

    a) So many other people vote in elections that it doesn't matter much whether I vote or not.

    b) People like me don't have any say about what the government does.

    c) Sometimes politics and government seem so complicated that a person like me can't really understand what's going on.

    d) Voting is the only way that people like me can have any say about how the government runs things.

    e) I don't think public officials care much about what people like me think.

48. Of all the ways of getting the news about government officials

and bureaus, which would you say you depend on the most: newspapers, radio, or television

49. Do you ever watch the University of Michigan Television Hour? (*If yes*) *a*) Have you seen it since last September?
       b) What did they take up the last time you saw it?
       c) About how often do you watch: regularly, once a month, or less

50. Do you have a television set?

51. One way in which some people in Detroit spend their time is in clubs and organizations. I would like you to look at this list of kinds of organizations and tell me if you belong to any organizations like labor unions, a church, and so on:

     Labor Unions: A local of some union
     A Church
     Church Connected Groups: Like a club connected with a church such as men's clubs, ladies' aid societies, Holy Name Societies, Missionary societies
     Fraternal Organizations or Lodges: Like the Masons, Knights of Columbus, Elks, Eastern Star
     Veterans Organizations: Like American Legion, Veterans of Foreign Wars
     Business or Civic Groups: Like Rotary, Kiwanis, Lions
     Parent-Teachers Associations
     Neighborhood Clubs or Community Centers
     Organizations of People of the Same Nationality Background: Like the Polish National Alliance, the B'Nai B'rith, the Steuben Society
     Sport Teams: Like bowling or baseball teams
     Professional Groups: Like the American Medical Association or a builders' association
     Political Clubs or Organizations
     Neighborhood Improvement Associations
     Women's Clubs
     Charitable and Welfare Organizations

(*If R belongs to any organizations*) *a*) What organizations or clubs do you belong to? (*List names of all organizations in full.*)
       b) We want to be sure we have all of the organizations you belong to. Are there any others that are not on this list? (*Add any mentioned.*)

52. All in all then, considering the good things and the bad, would you say that as a place to live the Detroit Area is:
     VERY BAD, BAD, FAIR, GOOD, VERY GOOD

We are also interested in possible changes in family size.

53. In your opinion what would be the ideal number of children for a young couple to have, if their standard of living is about like yours?

The following statement is a suggested form for transition to the personal data questions. Vary this in any way you think necessary.

Well, that completed the regular part of the interview. As I was telling you, we don't take the names of people on our surveys, but we do get a few facts about the people we talk to. I mean like occupation, age, income, and so on. We do this so we can compare the ideas of different people in different occupations, for example; or compare the ideas of younger people with those of older people, and so on.

CENSUS DATA

1. Race (by observation):   White   Negro   Other ....
                                                                (specify)

2. Sex (by observation):   Male   Female

3. Age (from face sheet): ....

4. Relationship to head of household (from face sheet): ....
....

5. Marital status (from face sheet): M.   S.   D.   Sep.   Wid.
   If married, divorced, separated, or widowed:
      5a) How long have you been married?   .... years
      5b) How many children have you had?   ....

6. How long have you lived in the Detroit area? (If needed, add: The Detroit area is any place in Wayne, Macomb, or Oakland counties.) ....
   If not entire life:
      6a) Where did you live most of your life before you came to the Detroit area?
      ....(Town)   ....(State)
      6b) Where were you born? .... (Town)
      .... (State)
      6c) Have you ever lived on a farm?   Yes   No
   If yes:
      6d) Where?   ....(State)
      6e) Between what ages?   .... to ....

7. How long have you lived in this house? ....

8. Do you own this house or are you renting
   Owns (or buying)   Rents   Other (explain)
   ----

9. What was the highest grade of school you completed?
   1   2   3   4   5   6   7   8   9   10   11   12
   More   If attended college:
   9a) How many years of college did you attend? ....

10. In grade or high school did you ever attend a parochial school?
    Yes   No
    If has children of school age or older:
    10a) Have your children ever attended a parochial grade or high school?   Yes   No

11. What is your religious preference? Catholic   Protestant
    Jewish   Other ....(specify)
    If Protestant:
    11a) What religious denomination is that? ....
                                                 (specify)

12. About how often do you usually attend religious services?
    Once a week?   Twice a month?   Once a month?
          A few times a year?   Never?

13. Have you or has anyone who lives here been in the service at any time since 1940?   Yes   No
    If yes:
    13a) Who is that? ....

14. Do any of your close relatives that do not live here work for the government?   Yes   No

15. Many people were out of work for sometime during the 1930–1940 period. Were you or was any member of the household in which you were living at that time unemployed and looking for work?   Yes   No

16. What was your total family income in 1953, considering all sources such as rents, profits, wages, interest, and so on?
    Under $1,000 $1,000–1,999 $2,000–2,999
    $3,000–3,999 $4,000–4,999 $5,000–5,999
    $6,000–6,999 $7,000–7,999 $8,000–8,999
    $9,000–9,999 $10,000 or more

Do not ask in one-adult households:

16a) How much of that was the income of the head of the family? ....

17. What is your occupation? (What sort of work do you do?)
.... (Lathe operator, stock clerk, housewife—
if unemployed or retired, ask what he or she does [did] when
working.) If retired, check here ....
If appropriate:

17a) What kind of business is that in? ....
(steel mill, grocery store, bank)

If employed:

17b) Do you work for yourself or for someone else?
Self   Someone else

Questions 18 to 24 refer to family head; if R is not head, use alternative wording. Also, if R is a widow or separated, obtain this information about her husband.

Ask only if R is not head:

18. What is your ....'s[1] (write in proper relationship)
occupation? (What sort of work does he do?) ....
.... (Lathe operator, stock clerk, etc.—
If unemployed or retired, also ask what he does [did] when working.) If retired, check here ....
If appropriate:

18a) What kind of business is that in? ....
(steel mill, grocery store, bank)

18b) Does he work for himself or someone else?
Self   Someone else

If head works for self:

19. How many people do you (does your head) normally employ? ....

If head works for someone else:

20. Do you (does he) have a job now?   Yes   No
If yes:
20a) How long have you (has he) worked at this place? ....
If no:
20b) How long have you (has he) been out of work? ....

[1]If R is wife of head, insert "husband." If R is father of head, insert "son," or
"daughter." If R is relative of head, insert proper relationship (cousin, aunt, etc.)

21. What was your (head's) occupation just after the end of the war in about the fall of 1945? ....
   If in service in the fall of 1945:
   21a) What was your (head's) occupation when he was first released from service? ....

22. What was your (head's) father's occupation when you were (your head was) growing up? ....
   (Lathe operator, stock clerk, etc.—if unemployed or retired or deceased, ask what he did when working.)
   If appropriate:
   22a) What kind of business was that in? ....
                        (steel mill, grocery store, bank)
   22b) Did he work for himself or someone else?
                        Self   Someone else
   If worked for self:
   22c) How many people did he normally employ? ....
   If farmer:
   22d) Did he usually own his farm, rent it, or work as a Farm Hand?   Own   Rent   Farm Hand

Ask anyone except Negroes:
   The forefathers of all Americans came from outside the United States originally.

23. What was the original nationality of your (head's) family on your (his) father's side? ....

24. Was your (head's) father born in the United States, Canada, or some other country?   U.S.   Canada   Other

CENSUS DATA ABOUT OTHER ADULTS IN DWELLING UNIT

1. (Enter race of informant):   White   Negro   Other..............
                                                  (specify)
Enter from face sheet:
2. Sex: Male   Female
3. Age: ....
4. Relationship to head: ....
5. Marital status: M.   S.   D.   Sep.   Wid.
Now about ....(relationship to head):
6. How long has he (she) lived in the Detroit area? (If needed, add: The Detroit area is any place in Wayne, Macomb, or

Oakland counties.) ....

If not entire life:

    6a) Where did he (she) live most of his (her) life before he (she) came here? ....(Town) ....

                                                  (State)

    6b) Where was he (she) born? ....(Town)..............................

                                                  (State)

    6c) Has he (she) ever lived on a farm? Yes No

If yes:

    6d) Where? .... (State)

    6e) Between what ages? .... to ....

9. What was the highest grade of school he (she) completed?

    1   2   3   4   5   6   7   8   9   10   11   12   More

    If attended college:

    9a) How many years did he (she) attend? ....

16. Does he (she) have an income apart from what you have already reported in your total family income? Yes No

    If yes:

    16a) How much was his (her) total income in 1953?

Under $1,000	$1,000–1,999	$2,000–2,999
$3,000–3,999	$4,000–4,999	$5,000–5,999
$6,000–6,999	$7,000–7,999	$8,000–8,999
$9,000–9,999	$10,000 or more	

Do not ask questions 17, 17a, or 17b for the head if already ascertained.

17. What is his (her) occupation? (What sort of work does he (she) do?) ....

(Lathe operator, stock clerk, etc.—if unemployed or retired, also ask what he does (did) when working.) If retired, check here.........

If appropriate:

    17a) What kind of business is that in? ....

                                         (steel mill, grocery store, bank)

    17b) Does he work for himself or someone else?

            Self   Someone else

APPENDIX C

SOCIAL CHARACTERISTICS OF THE SAMPLE

Sex	Number	Per Cent
Male	360	47
Female	404	53
	764	100

Race	Number	Per Cent
White	658	86
Negro	106	14
	764	100

Age	Number	Per Cent
21-29	174	23
30-39	214	28
40-49	142	18
50-59	113	15
60 and over	121	16
	764	100

Home Ownership	Number	Per Cent
Family owns home	511	67
Family rents	243	32
Not ascertained	10	1
	764	100

Religious Preference	Number	Per Cent
Protestant	428	56
Catholic	291	38
Jewish	21	3
Other	10	1
No preference	14	2
	764	100

Education	Number	Per Cent
Some elementary school	133	17
Completed elementary school	105	14
Some high school	173	24
Completed high school	236	31
Some or completed college	109	15
Not ascertained	8	1
	764	100

Occupation of Family Head	Number	Per Cent
Professional, technical	71	9
Manager, official or proprietor .	98	13
Clerical, sales.................	89	12
Craftsman, foreman	214	28
Operators	186	24
Private household workers, service workers, laborers	77	10
Not ascertained	29	4
	764	100

Social Class	Number	Per Cent
Working class—lower	250	33
Working class—upper	207	27
Middle class—lower	186	24
Middle class—upper[1]	106	14
Not ascertained	15	2
	764	100

Total Family Income	Number	Per Cent
Under $2,000	49	6
$2,000–$3,999	107	14
$4,000–$4,999	104	14
$5,000–$5,999	120	15
$6,000–$6,999	82	11
$7,000–$7,999	83	11
$8,000–$9,999	91	12
$10,000 or over	96	13
Not ascertained	32	4
	764	100

Length of Residence in Detroit Area	Number	Per Cent
Less than 5 years	90	12
6 to 10 years	85	11
11 to 15 years	64	8
16 to 20 years	42	6
21 to 25 years	37	5
26 to 30 years	76	10
31 or more years	139	18
All life in Detroit area	229	30
Not ascertained	2	...
	764	100

[1]Includes one per cent classified in upper class.

APPENDIX D

OPERATIONALIZATION OF SOCIAL CLASS

EACH family unit in which an interview was taken was assigned "membership" in an objective-type social class. These assignments were determined primarily on the basis of the occupation of the head of the family unit of which the respondent was a member. Thus, where respondent and the head of the household were not the same person, the class position of respondent was that of head of the household.

Occupations were coded according to the Bureau of the Census occupation code[1] and a class designation was made as follows (exceptions will be noted below):

Class	Census Occupation Code
8. Lower upper class	O. & 2. Select professional, managerial and entrepreneurial workers
6. Upper middle class	O. Professional, technical and kindred workers
	2. Managers, officials and proprietors except farm
5. Lower middle class	3. Clerical and kindred workers
	4. Sales workers
3. Upper working class	5. Craftsmen, foremen and kindred workers
2. Lower working class	6. Operatives (semi-skilled) and kindred workers
	7. Service workers
	9. Laborers
.. Class not ascertained	.. Occupation not ascertained

While the assignment of class by occupation classification was highly standardized, it was felt desirable to include criteria other than occupation. The chief criteria for these adaptations were income, occupation prestige when inconsistent with the

[1] U. S. Department of Commerce, Bureau of the Census. *1950 Census of Population. Alphabetical Index of Occupations and Industries* (Washington: Gov. Printing Office, 1950).

general occupation class code group, education, ethnic background, and, in a small number of cases, area of residence. Other criteria are not specified herein, often being applicable to single cases whose idiosyncracies seemed to the coders to justify singular treatment; however, they were introduced only as conceptually consistent with the adaptations indicated below.

Up-coding

From occupation group O: entrepreneurs, managers, and professionals with incomes of more than $10,000 were coded "8" (lower upper class) when (a) the specific details of their occupations indicated especially high prestige (e.g., gentleman-farmer-rentier), or (b) area of residence (e.g., Grosse Pointe), or (c) interviewer comments, or any combination of such or similar elements, pointed to status higher than appropriate for coding "6" (upper middle class).

From occupation group 2: same as in regarding occupation group O.

From occupation group 4: salesmen making more than $10,000 coded upper middle class.

From occupation group 5: craftsmen engaged in especially high-skill and high-prestige employments (e.g., lithographer, optical grinding specialist) and with commensurately high income (more than $10,000 in several cases although, rarely, in the $7,000 category) were put into the lower middle class (code "5").

From occupation group 6: operatives having high income were up-coded to "3" (upper working class) if other status data seemed to support such a revision.

From occupation group 7: service workers with high incomes, or self-employed (e.g., bartender running his own tavern), were up-coded to "3" (upper working class) or "5" (lower middle class) as the other evidence warranted. Similarly, government-employed "service" workers, private police, etc.

As indicated already for occupation group 7, the occupation code classifies various employments in skill categories even if they are pursued entrepreneurially. Such occupations, from groups 3, 4, and 5 as well as from group 7, were up-coded as appropriate to income and occupational prestige.

Down-coding

From occupation group O: public school teachers, nurses, draftsmen, lab technicians, non-college graduate engineers and accountants, fundamentalist, evangelical and part-time ministers, and similar classifications were put into the lower middle class (code "5").

From occupation group 2: managers, officials and proprietors, except farm, with incomes of less than $10,000, fewer than six employees, non-executive occupational roles, or low prestige occupations, as variously appropriate, were put into the lower middle class (code "5").

From occupation groups 3, 4, and 5: recent Negro migrants in these groups were put into the lower working class when other data seem to support such an adaptation.

CONSISTENCY BETWEEN SOCIAL CLASS POSITION
AND OCCUPATIONAL POSITION

Class	Direction of Shift from Occupation Position to Class Position			
	None	Up	Down	Total
Lower working...........	243		7	250
Upper working...........	194	9	4	207
Lower middle............	77	36	73	186
Upper middle............	83	15		98
Upper..................	8			8
Not ascertained	15			15
Total	620	60	84	764

The data above shows that the largest number of shifts were made downward from upper middle to lower middle and upward from the working to the lower middle class.

Three persons participated in assigning class, so that each assignment was made by two persons independently. When differences could not be compromised clearly in line with the adjustment principles outlined above—i.e., when crystallization among the component elements of class assignment was low—the lower of the independently assigned classes was designated for the final coding.

INDEX